AF126667

Great Railway Eras
RETURN TO BLAENAU
1970-82

Vic Mitchell and Allan Garraway

MP Middleton Press

Cover picture: *This headboard made an important statement to the world on a number of occasions in the late 1970s. The photograph is from 25th June 1977, the date of the official opening to Llyn Ystradau.* **Merddin Emrys** *is also carrying the "Golden Spade". Passenger service began here on 8th July. (Norman Gurley/Ffestiniog Railway Company)*

> **Dedicated to Leonard Heath-Humphrys, who in his late teens, had the courage, foresight and vision to call a meeting in Bristol in 1951 which led to the formation of the Festiniog Railway Society. It has brought pleasure and fulfillment to countless enthusiasts and professionals. Sadly, Leonard died nine months before the 50th anniversary of this event.**

Published April 2001

ISBN 1 901706 64 8

© Middleton Press, 2001

Design   Deborah Esher
Typesetting   Barbara Mitchell

Published by
    Middleton Press
    Easebourne Lane
    Midhurst, West Sussex
    GU29 9AZ
Tel: 01730 813169
Fax: 01730 812601

Printed & bound by Biddles Ltd,
    Guildford and Kings Lynn

CONTENTS

	Page		
1970	8	1977	57
1971	15	1978	60
1972	22	1979	63
1973	28	1980	66
1974	35	1981	76
1975	42	1982	83
1976	50		

INDEX TO FR LOCATIONS

	Page
Blaenau Ffestiniog	68, 73, 74, 75, 79, 83, 86-94
Boston Lodge	18, 28, 63, 69, 78
Dduallt	8, 15, 19, 21, 32, 37, 44, 51
Glan-y-Pwll	33, 34, 42, 54, 84, 85
Llyn Ystradau	7, 44, 45, 56
Minffordd	12, 29, 38, 39, 50
Moelwyn Tunnel	6, 30, 47, 55, 58
Penrhyn	57
Portmadoc Harbour	10, 14, 20, 25, 32, 35, 36, 41, 82
Rhiw Goch	40
Tan-y-Bwlch	11, 17
Tanygrisiau	48, 49, 53, 61, 62, 64, 66, 71, 72, 80, 81

Pictures included mainly for their technical interest are not listed.

ACKNOWLEDGEMENTS

Our gratitude goes to Norman Langridge for scanning the magazine extracts; to Jim Hewett and to Arthur Lambert for aiding our memories on factual matters; to David and Susan Salter for proof reading our text and to Moyra Garraway and Barbara Mitchell for tolerating our prolonged absences during our recent periods of "holiday" together. We thank you all most sincerely.

INTRODUCTION

This volume is intended to illustrate some of the aspects of the final stages of the Festiniog Railway revival seen only by a few in most cases. All the photographs are from the camera of Allan Garraway, who was general manager throughout the period covered by this publication. It is intended as a sequel to *Festiniog in the Sixties*, but goes beyond the next decade to include the restoration of the entire route.

The extracts from the *Festiniog Railway Magazine* are limited to selected news items that we consider to be of special interest, a consideration also used in selecting the photographs. Some of the prophecies were not to be fulfilled however. The annual locomotive mileages were published each Spring and so appear in that position in the magazine extracts. References to engine oil being required no longer apply.

As in our two previous albums, we are assuming that readers have some knowledge of the line and the reason for only one "F" being in its title for most of the era covered. For those wishing to seek more background information, we would suggest reference to *Branch Lines around Portmadoc 1923-46* and *Branch Lines around Porthmadog 1954-94* (Middleton Press).

I. The FR is shown in 1978 with the spiral at Dduallt complete and the new route open up to Tanygrisiau. The dashed line on the right was used by BR trains carrying nuclear fuel flasks.

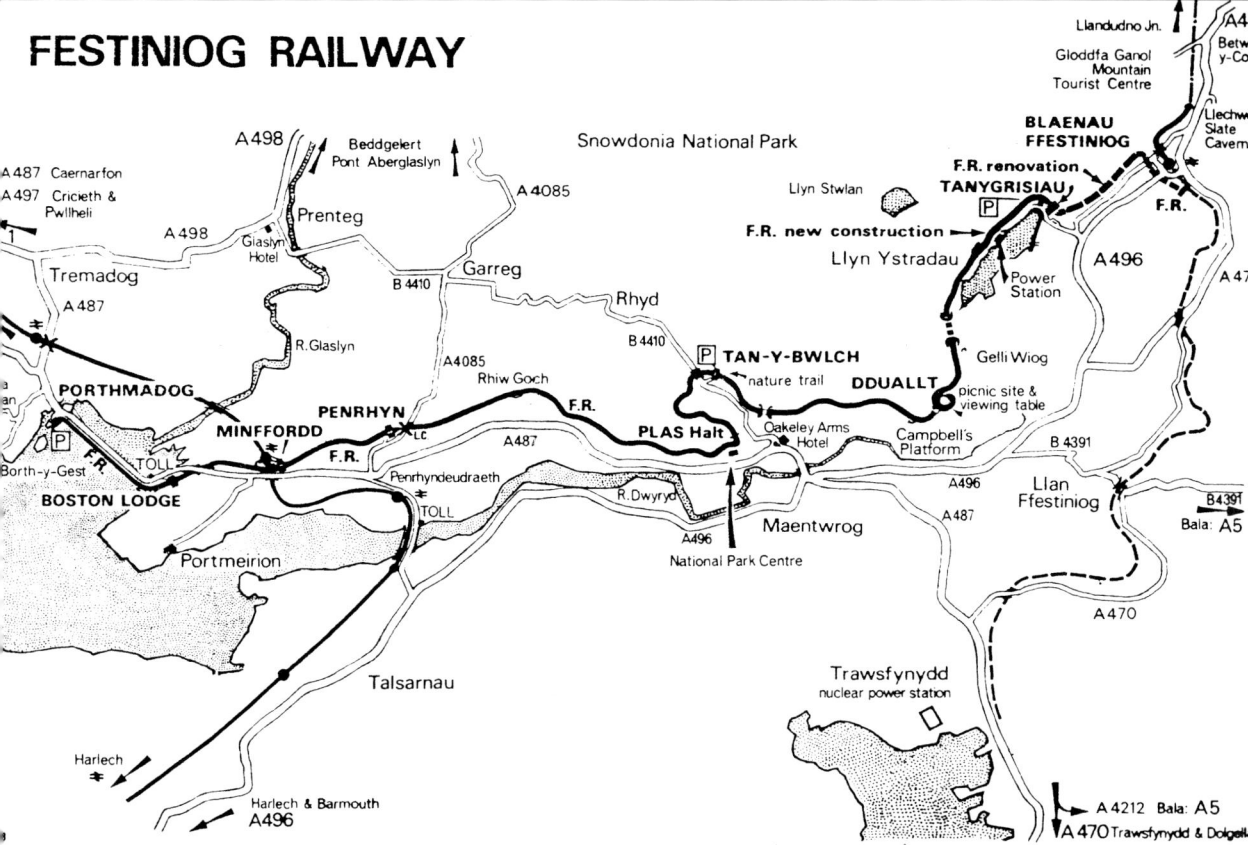

FESTINIOG RAILWAY
Winter Timetable 1974-75

23rd September, 1974 to 23rd March, 1975
(DAILY SERVICES recommence 26th March)

	DAILY Mon., 23 Sept. to Thurs., 31 Oct. (except Fridays, 11, 18, 25 Oct.)			EVERY SAT. & SUN., 2 Nov. to 15 Dec.	SAT. & SUN. 21–22 Dec. SO	BOXING DAY 26 Dec.		DAILY 27 Dec. to 1 Jan. Also Sat.-Sun., 4–5 Jan.	EVERY SAT. & SUN., 15 Feb. to 23 Mar.
PORTHMADOG	1115	1315	1515	1415	1330 1415 1915	1315	1515	1415	1415
BOSTON LODGE	RQ	RQ	RQ	RQ		RQ	RQ	RQ	RQ
MINFFORDD	1126	1326	1526	1426	CHRISTMAS	1326	1526	1426	1426
PENRHYN	1132	1332	1532	1432	EXCURSIONS	1332	1532	1432	1432
TAN-Y-BWLCH arr.	1150	1350	1550	1450	Details	1350	1550	1450	1450
dep.	1155	1355	1555	1455	see below	1355	1555	1455	1455
DDUALLT	1205	1405	1605	1505		1405	1605	1505	1505
DDUALLT	1218	1418	1618	1518		1418	1618	1518	1518
TAN-Y-BWLCH arr.	1228	1428	1628	1528		1428	1628	1528	1528
dep.	1230	1430	1630	1530		1430	1630	1530	1530
PENRHYN	1249	1449	1649	1549		1449	1649	1549	1549
MINFFORDD	1255	1455	1655	1555		1455	1655	1555	1555
BOSTON LODGE	RQ	RQ	RQ	RQ	SO	RQ	RQ	RQ	RQ
PORTHMADOG	1305	1505	1705	1605	1615 1645 2105	1505	1705	1605	1605

RQ – Calls on request.   SO – Saturday Only — Off peak fares apply (3rd Class 70p, 1st Class £1·10)

Although every possible effort will be made to ensure running as timetable, the Festiniog Railway will not guarantee advertised connections in the event of breakdown or other obstruction of services.

SATURDAY AND SUNDAY, 21/22 DECEMBER
Special Father Christmas Excursions will operate as follows:
Porthmadog depart 1330 and 1415 (arrive back 1615 and 1645, respectively). Father Christmas will meet the trains at Tan-y-Bwlch with presents for the children.

Fares: 3rd Class. Adult Return £1·10. Children (under 14) 55p. FR Society Members 50p. 1st class 40p supplement in all cases. Seasonal snacks from buffet car optional extra. Advance booking advised on these trains.

PRINCIPAL FARES ON ALL TRAINS EXCEPT EXCURSIONS
Porthmadog to Dduallt: 3rd Class return 90p. 1st Class return £1·20. Children under 14 half fare. Buffet and observation cars on all trains.

PLEASE NOTE. Whilst the Company continues to use steam traction on the majority of its trains, it reserves the right to use diesel locomotives where necessary during the winter service.

SPECIAL PARTIES AND PRIVATE CHARTER TRAINS BY ARRANGEMENT
Festiniog Railway Company, Porthmadog, Gwynedd. Tel. Porthmadog 2384

 *One of the Great Little Trains of Wales*

T. Stephenson & Sons Ltd., Printers, Prescot, Merseyside

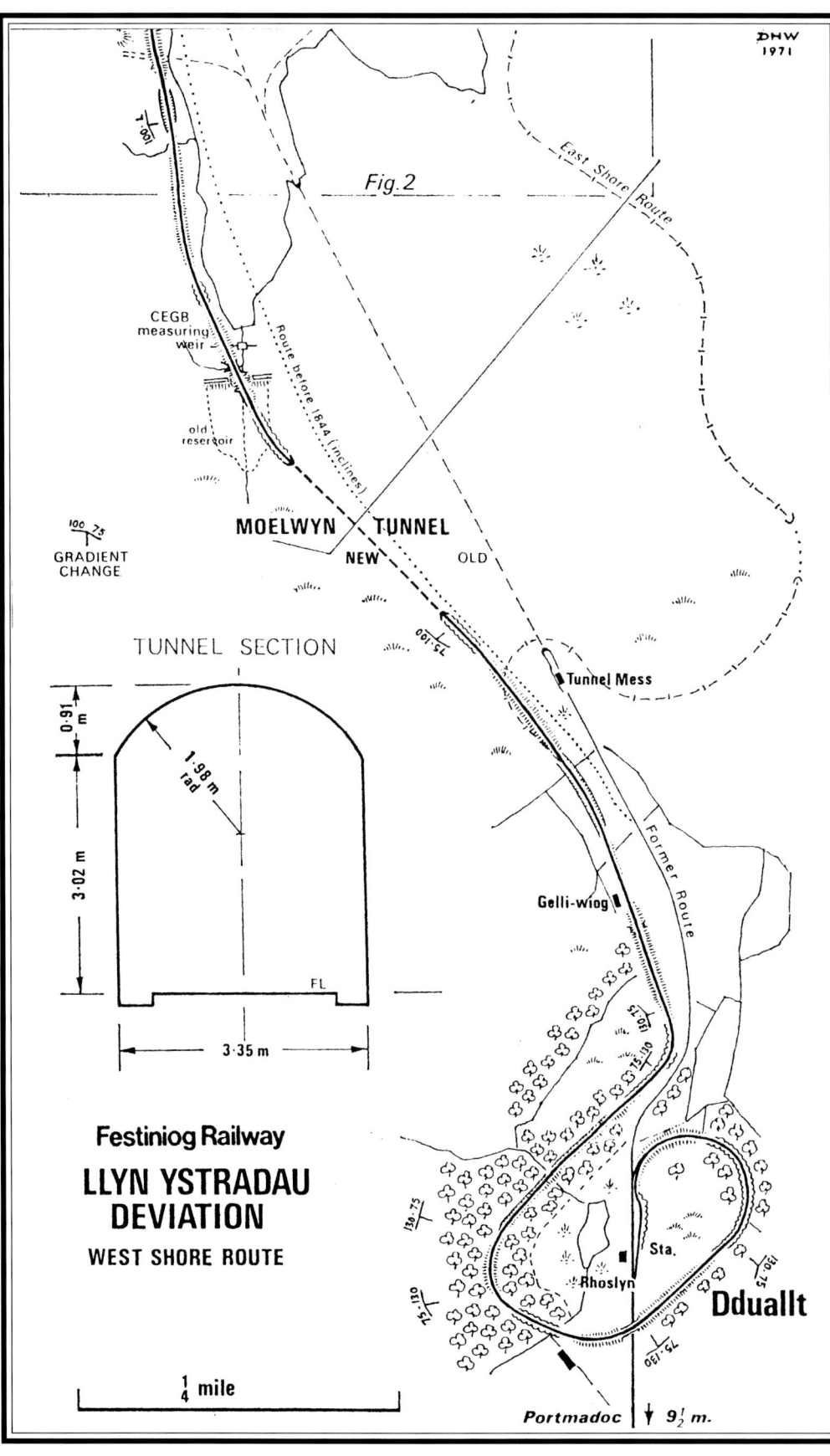

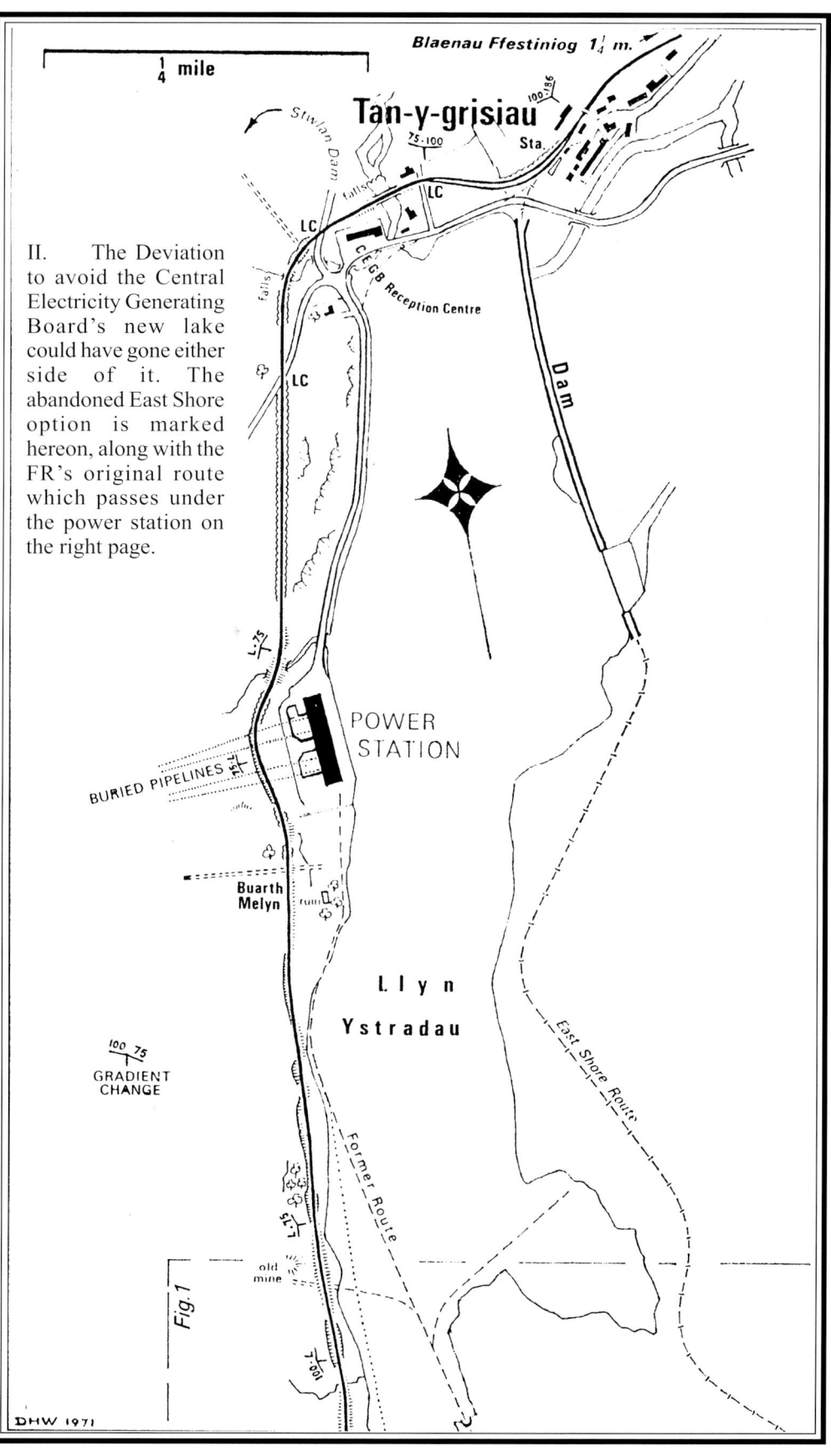

1970

Spring 1970

The first lorry load of Jarrah sleepers arrived from Liverpool on 12th January, and relaying commenced at Rhiw Plas immediately. In all, 72 rail lengths were relayed, from Boston Lodge Halt to the start of Cemetery Cutting. Apart from final topping up of ballast, the work here was finished on 1st March, one day behind schedule. Concurrently, work had been done from time to time at the bridge by Nazareth Chapel, Penrhyn, in conjunction with the Council. The big day was 23rd January, when a fifteen-ton road mobile crane was used to lift the two four-ton and two two-ton concrete beams off bogie wagons and into position.

Throughout January and February, Moelwyn was sub-shedded at Minffordd goods shed, and handled a multiplicity of loads between Minffordd yard and the rail-heads at Rhiw Plas and Nazareth.

The Jarrah sleepers have proved well up to expectations; in spite of their considerable weight (approx. 100lb each) they are clean and easy to handle, whilst their undoubted strength and durability encourages care and pride in their use. It may not be generally realised that the milling of Jarrah (Eucalyptus marginata) is one of the principal industries of Western Australia, where it grows on vast ironstone ridges. It is ideal timber for railway use, and is preferred to concrete in many parts of the world.

70.1 Work had started on the southern part of the Deviation, long before the route around the lake had been decided. A view from March 1970 shows that the loop at Dduallt was still unballasted on the first embankment of the Deviation.

Weekend work has been put in at Tan-y-Bwlch, installing colour light home signals as a temporary measure pending the introduction of full mechanical signalling. Similar work is being done at Minffordd where, at the top end of the station, the up line catch point has been interlocked with the top points. Control is still from the lever frame alongside the points rather than from the frame under the station awning.

The New Year was celebrated in fine style, with First Sod week-end attracting so many that all our available bunk accommodation was inadequate. Even the ample floor of the Mess was littered with sleeping bodies. During the following week a party of Westminster School boys stayed on with the intention of putting the finishing touches to the pillars of Rhoslyn Bridge. This was frustrated largely by the frosty weather, though a start was made at the end of the week.

Members are reminded that the Festiniog Railway Company is an accredited British Rail Travel Agency. Tickets can be supplied for virtually any British Rail journey, and we take pride in dealing promptly with all orders and enquiries. To avoid anxiety, please allow time for postal delays.

70.2 The old bolster wagons were refurbished and are seen outside Boston Lodge Works prior to their employment on the biggest track laying programme on the FR that century.

Summer 1970

Alterations to the trackwork at the top end of Dduallt station were completed to schedule, and by Easter locos were using part of the deviation, albeit just a few yards, whilst running round. Sufficient track has been laid to permit works vehicles to be parked on the spiral, and materials are stacked in readiness for the laying of some 400 yards of track during July and August when the volunteer labour force is at its strongest. The aim is to stop just short of Rhoslyn bridge, where special decking is to be erected to facilitate the positioning of pre-stressed concrete beams next winter.

The colour light signal scheme at Tan-y-Bwlch was put into operation on 16th May. It has been installed as an interim measure pending completion of the full signalling scheme.

The three-aspect signals are operated from a panel installed in the old station building and are interlocked with the ground frames. Provided the road is set correctly, pressing the appropriate button either at the panel or at the ground frame (where remote operation buttons are provided) gives either a green for normal line operation or yellow for "wrong line" running. The passage of a train over a treadle automatically replaces the appropriate signal to danger.

Major Olver of the Railway Inspectorate, who visited the Railway on 12th April, complimented the S. & T. Dept. on the work carried out. The Ministry regard the installation as a temporary one giving enhanced operating safety necessary because of the intensive service now being operated.

On 10th April a double ceremony took place at Dduallt, with a number of Festiniog Railway Company Directors and other officials in attendance. The 15.15 train was smartly turned out, with *Earl of Merioneth* at the head and the two original iron-framed bogie coaches, Nos. 15 and 16, in the formation. No. 16 had in fact only left shops that afternoon, after being equipped with its permanent roller bearing bogies, and after inspecting and admiring the standard of the interior fittings Mr. Pegler officially inaugurated the coach into service, thus closing the fifteen-year task of restoring the surviving Festiniog Railway passenger rolling stock.

The assembled company then made their way to the top of the hill in the centre of the spiral loop, where a plinth has been constructed of stone sets lifted from the approach road to Minffordd Exchange Sidings. This provides the bed for a beautifully engraved slate slab indicating the height and direction of the principal peaks and other points of interest visible from the hill. The General Manager then introduced the donors, Mr. and Mrs. Walker of London, and Mrs. Walker unveiled the orientation table. The ceremony over, the slab was removed for safe keeping, pending arrival of a vandal-proof protective cover.

70.3 At the opposite end of the line, it was business as usual, plus an occasional special train as seen in June 1970. This one was to mark the centenary of the Fairlie engine trials. The town retained its old name and the station still had a separate goods shed, although it had served as a garage for the GM's car.

70.4   Two Americans were recorded at work in August 1970. Baldwin-built *Moelwyn* assists Alco-built *Mountaineer* past Tan-y-Bwlch cafe. The siding points (left) acted as catch points, a feature sadly lacking at several recent disaster sites in England.

70.5   At the opposite end of Tan-y-Bwlch station, later the same day, *Moelwyn* is seen returning with the Dduallt shuttle train. The historic four-wheelers had often been used as adaptor vehicles prior to 1939, having different types of couplings on opposite ends.

Autumn 1970

July saw *Mountaineer* involved in two unfortunate incidents, the first when she collided with *Earl* and *Linda* in the works and the second when her rear (chilled cast iron) pony truck flange shed a segment only a few days before a new set of wheels was scheduled to be fitted. She returned to Boston Lodge as a 2-6-0T, and was then returned to traffic for a few days as an 0-6-2T, the new wheels then being fitted under the front. *Earl of Merioneth* and *Blanche* both suffered seasonal ills, but three engines have always been available and timekeeping has generally been good in spite of the extra complications created by the Dduallt shuttle.

The first notable traffic event of the Autumn service was a BR public excursion from Manchester on Sunday 6th September, giving a full round trip (Minffordd-Dduallt-Portmadoc-Minffordd) on the F.R. at quite an attractive all-in fare. After the driver of a type 4 diesel had vehemently insisted at Crewe that he was booked to work through to Pwllheli (Barmouth bridge and all) and then one of the two replacement type 2s (no, we don't know the latest classification) had burst into flames, the F.R. found itself running the special *between* the 14.00 and the 14.45 service trains. In the end, the 160 excursionists had an entertaining wait at Tan-y-Bwlch while the 15.10 down train crossed

---

70.6 Lack of sufficient carriage sheds was a problem partially resolved by the modification of slate storage sheds in Minffordd Yard. This involved raising the massive roofs bodily and then raising the height of the supporting piers.

theirs, which in turn was combined with the 14.45 up for the rest of the journey, giving the second double-headed twelve coacher of the year.

The operation and economics of the Tan-y-Bwlch to Dduallt shuttle service have created much interest and warrant examination in detail. The shuttle train (more often known as the Dduallt Diddy) consisted of *Moelwyn*, quarrymen's coach No. 8, bug-boxes Nos. 5 and 6 and brake van No. 2. It ran on Mondays to Thursdays as directed by Control, leaving Tan-y-Bwlch immediately a main train arrived at Dduallt and running into the loop at Dduallt when the main train engine had run round its train. The main train would then leave three minutes earlier than shown in the public timetable, to be followed by the shuttle on clearing the section. By the time the shuttle ran into Tan-y-Bwlch the down main train had normally vacated the down platform and the up train had taken water and was ready to leave for Dduallt. The shuttle engine would then have ten minutes for running round and servicing, before leaving for Dduallt again. The working timetable permitted a maximum of nine up shuttles and eight down (the balancing working being combined with a main train), giving a grand total of 43 workings between Tan-y-Bwlch and Dduallt. In fact the shuttle rarely used its first and last paths, but early morning and evening staff workings with Col. Campbell's Simplex often made up the number.

Winter 1970

With five different steam locomotives being seen at the head of service trains during October and November, interest has tended to centre more on the motive power than on the passenger loadings, especially as a miserable October was followed by the wettest November ever recorded in parts of Wales. Nevertheless, passenger figures have compared favourably with the autumn figures last year, and have justified efforts made to boost the results with some extra trains. Publicity for *Linda's* oil-burning trial runs on non-operating days invited passengers to participate on a "mystery tour" basis, and even a diesel-hauled special to convey the Railway Letter Service Christmas issue first day covers on 25th November was advertised locally. Trains were run with a fair measure of support on 5-6th December and good turn-outs were expected for Santa Claus specials on 19-20th December; 250 advance bookings were received for the Sunday train.

The busiest day of the autumn was Saturday, 3rd October, when the T.R.P.S. day excursion from London brought 450 visitors to the two railways in addition to those attending the T.R.P.S. Annual General Meeting. Half the visitors arrived at Minffordd in quite the longest and smartest BR rake ever to be seen there, and joined an *Earl of Merioneth* hauled special via Dduallt to Tan-y-Bwlch. Here they changed places with the other contingent, who had arrived by coach from Abergynolwyn, and the procedure was reversed. The weather was good and the organisation first class; it was a great day for the narrow gauge image.

A month later *Merddin Emrys* was in the limelight, and after cautious outings on 1st and 7th November a real test was provided on Sunday, 8th, with a twelve coach train and a greasy wet rail. The passengers had quite a thrilling run, and those who knew anything at all about railways must have been impressed by the obviously excellent steaming of the new boiler.

The year's passenger journey figure is expected to be in the region of 352,000 when all the returns have been accumulated.

Much time has been spent at Minffordd during the autumn and the conversion of the old Maenofferen/Davies Bros. slate shed/hen battery for winter carriage storage is well advanced. The roof lifting operation went smoothly and the end and side walls have been virtually completed. It now remains for the sliding end doors to be installed and a traversing stub point giving access to the four roads (each accommodating two cars) to be laid. It is proposed to deal similarly with the smaller shed alongside in the autumn of 1971 and to roof the gap between the two sheds, to give a whole covered complex accommodating 14 vehicles.

Also at Minffordd repairs to the P.W. Dept's Nissen hut and the Foreman's office have been completed. At Boston Lodge, work on the S. & T. telephone exchange room, a new oil store and the No. 2 machine shop is all completed. Two major projects for the winter months are the provision of a new sales store above the Ladies' room at Harbour Station and the conversion of part of the pattern loft at Boston Lodge for works office accommodation.

While the various construction details of the West Side route continue to be debated, estimated and cartographed, work continues with undiminishing vigour at various sites on the spiral; so undiminished, in fact, that a London party established a new week-end record of 103 skips filled and tipped on 14-15th November.

The major project for the winter is the provision of the permanent decking for Rhoslyn bridge. The old temporary decking was removed during October and preparations started for handling the 16 tons of delicate prestressed concrete beams - delicate, that is, until safely in position and doing the job they were designed for. Fortunately the appeal for specialised assistance published in the last *Magazine* did not go unheeded, and by the time the beams were delivered, exactly on schedule at 9 a.m. -26th November in Minffordd yard, an elaborate system of bogies and rails was assembled at Dduallt to sling, roll and coax the beams into their correct positions. The beams were hauled to Dduallt by *Merddin Emrys* on 28th November, and the installation operations were scheduled to commence on 4th January.

70.7   *Britomart* was out in the rain for a childrens party in December 1970. The purists sniffed at Santa Specials, but they soon became a lifeline for all preserved railways. Did the FR pioneer them?

Spring 1971

We have not previously had trains to report on in the Spring *Magazine,* but the success of the Father Christmas specials on 19-20th December would seem to indicate that these will be a regular feature in future. What started as a Saturday afternoon outing for a Penrhyn church party eventually ran as three trains, one on the Saturday and two on Sunday, carrying well over 400 passengers. Most of them were children from the Portmadoc and Penrhyn areas, all of whom received a present from Father Christmas at Tan-y-Bwlch, while refreshments and a film show were laid on for the booked parties. A local pop group provided entertainment during the intervals when *Merddin Emrys* was not blowing off, and if the sun had not been shining so brightly Tan-y-Bwlch illuminations would have caught the eye. It was a great public relations exercise, and all credit goes to the staff and volunteers who decorated the trains and wrapped up more than 300 presents in addition to the more normal preparations for running out-of-season trains.

Even without the boost from Santa it has been the traffic department's busiest winter, as trains were run at weekly or fortnightly intervals for *Linda's* oil-fired trials. As performances improved longer trains were called for, and with some coaches tucked away for the winter and others in shops closed van No. 9 and piped bogie open No. 63 gave the train a real mixed-traffic appearance. The requirements of the P.W. Dept. finally won the day, however, and "winter" on the Railway began on 16th February. Prior to that, two-coach *Moelwyn*-hauled mail trains had run, with "last day covers" and 30 passengers on Sunday, 14th February, and first day covers and a handful of passengers on D-Day.

1971

71.1 The Deviation spiral's flyover, known as Rhoslyn Bridge, was created during January, using 15 beams, simple lifting tackle, much ingenuity and a good coordinated team, mainly of volunteers. The weather was indifferent, particularly for photography.

The winter's programme hinged on the arrival of the consignment of jarrah sleepers from Australia and as the ship concerned twice disappeared from the Liverpool shipping arrival estimates there were fears that little relaying would be done. Fortunately the timbers were handled quickly once the ship arrived, and were on the Railway within four days. Relaying started at Tro Bagl (between Plas Halt and Tan-y-Bwlch) on 18th February, and at Gwyndy Bank ten days later. At the latter location the 75 lb/yard flat bottom rail (ex-Rhymney and Barry Railways) had already been Thermit welded into approx. 84 ft. lengths.

It is often claimed, when other departments on the Railway are short of volunteers, that the pioneering nature of deviation work is its main attraction. That may well be true, but conversely progress is unexcitingly slow and monotonous. This report could easily have been written last autumn and it would not be difficult to write notes for next winter's *Magazines* at the same time. To the deviationists the big news is not that the concrete beams of Rhoslyn Bridge were erected as planned during January, or that Dragon has been linked with Rosary-both were inevitable-but that some boys are currently helping Police with their enquiries into a series of break-ins at Moelwyn Mess; items stolen during 1970 have been recovered.

In the summer we shall be reporting the completion of a further stage in the building of Rhoslyn Bridge, involving the application of some 30 tons of ready-mixed concrete, transported from Tan-y-Bwlch in Hudson wagons lined with polythene sheeting.

The Snowdonia National Park authorities must sometimes wonder whether they are supposed to conserve the area for the people or from the people. If there isn't someone wanting to carpet it with caravans or dig it up, there's someone else wanting to grow telegraph poles on it or flood it – or less spectacularly but more importantly, someone else again, in his innocent thousands, who just wants to come and look at it. Moorland can take just so many feet, narrow roads just so many wheels; beyond is ruin. A fact long recognised in ecological circles is that if you look for the least damaging means of introducing large numbers of people into wild and fragile scenery, the answer is a narrow-gauge railway.

If God meant us to see Snowdonia, He would have given us flanged wheels and a chimney

The Festiniog Railway bisects the National Park exactly – indeed, it passes through the grounds of the National Park Centre at Plas Tan-y-Bwlch. Primarily a slate-carrying line, it fell derelict in time to avoid becoming British Railways and was rescued by enthusiasts in 1954. Since then the railway has been steadily renovated and restored to the standards of its Victorian zenith, when its engineering ingenuity and professional sparkle set off a miniature world boom in narrow-gauge lines; so that now services operate from Portmadoc over the whole redeemable bottom length of the original track. Above this a section has been lost under the Ffestiniog pumped-storage electricity scheme; and to regain the hill terminal at Blaenau Ffestiniog a deviation line has been put in hand. Half a mile of this has already been built, almost entirely by voluntary, unpaid labour.

Tourism makes a dull crusader for Celtic prosperity: no Welshman will ever die for its flag. But when mineral veins expire, construction projects terminate, marginal agriculture flags, when fringe factories feel the frost and the tap is shut off for subsidised transport, tourism remains, humbly bringing gold without strings. Very shortly, with present trends, Merioneth's only public transport will be steam-operated narrow-gauge trains.

Those who know Snowdonia know that the Festiniog is no mere railway: it appeals on all levels. The Vale of Ffestiniog, through which it runs, was once described by Bertrand Russell as "like an old apocalyptic engraving of Paradise". Paradise may be minimally peopled, but it is surely not without railways. Come and see.

Telephone Portmadoc (0766) 2384

Rheilffordd Ffestiniog / Festiniog Railway

Summer 1971

The political and literary weekly the *New Statesman* recently organised a competition for advertisements which best "demonstrate the advertiser's awareness of his wider social responsibilities". Three prizes were offered, of £250, £150 and £100 and free insertion of the winning advertisements in the *New Statesman* (readership 400,000).

This contest attracted phenomenal interest and there were 163 entries from companies and corporations such as I.B.M., Philips, the Gas Council and Green Shield Stamps, and non-commercial bodies such as Oxfam and the Wildfowl Trust. Most of the big national advertising agencies were involved.

The winners were *The Ecologist Magazine*, the British Steel Corporation (steel crash barriers) and Harry Moss (London) Ltd. (car head rests) and an entry by *Festiniog Railway Magazine* Editor D. H. Wilson, on behalf of the Festiniog Railway (narrow-gauge railway travel) was awarded a specially created fourth prize of £50 and a free insertion. The cheque was handed over by the Editor of the *New Statesman*, Richard Crossman, at a reception in London and the free insertion of the advertisement (worth £270) was due to appear in the *New Statesman* on 18th June. It is reproduced (shrunk to nearly half size) opposite.

Locomotive mileages for 1970

	1970	Total under present administration
Prince	nil	40,287
Earl of Merioneth	5,940	43,429
Merddin Emrys	151	12,075
Linda	6,022	30,400
Blanche	7,868	31,915
Mountaineer	5,948	11,878
Moelwyn	1,819	22,800
Upnor Castle	364	1,532
Tyke	nil	180
Alistair	574	2,446
Simplex tractor	1,845	6,996
Wickham Trolley	nil	10,187

The start to the 1971 season was the smoothest on record. Easter can usually be relied upon to provide some interesting happenings, but the augmented train service coped with all offering traffic and the exclusive use of oil-burning *Linda* and the Fairlies completely eliminated the forestry fire risk in spite of the dry conditions.

As each of the oil-fired engines will be consuming something like 1,000 gallons of gas oil per week during the peak season, mobile storage of the fuel has created some problems. Several temporary tank wagons were assembled and the four-compartment ex-road tank which has been stored at Minffordd for some time was mounted on a Hudson bogie chassis and had its first rendezvous with a road tanker on 27th May.

On the same day buffet car No. 14 was handed over to the traffic department, resplendent in red livery. All 18 bogie coaches were then in service in red livery, many of them with the new style black ends. Work had started on the construction of the prototype toast-rack coach on a Hudson bogie chassis, inevitably referred to as the "bogie bugbox".

It is rare for deviation progress to be described as spectacular, but even the most staid and weatherbeaten deviationists have expressed surprise at the speed at which Dragon Site is approaching New Moon-and vice versa. These sites will continue to be the bread-and-butter jobs for the summer camp in July and August as well as the weekend parties throughout the year, but the work may well tend to become a matter of working sideways, widening and trimming the cuttings. Much fill will be required for New Moon embankment long after the two cuttings have joined, and as the strata of the rock is favourable the cuttings will probably be opened out to a shelf-like formation, which will be spectacular even by F.R. standards.

71.2 A noteworthy and photogenic occasion was the presence of all the company's passenger rolling stock at Tan-y-Bwlch on 11th June.

Autumn 1971

At mid June we were 11% up on 1970, but then it started raining. We like it hot in June, when the children are at school and there's not too much competition from the beaches, but the rain obviously kept many people at home. Then the sun shone for the whole of July, and parents who were perhaps a little short of cash were very happy to spend the whole of their holiday on the beach, leaving us only 2% up at the end of July. That 2% was quickly washed away early in August, but things started to improve in the middle of the month-on the 18th to be exact. Monday and Tuesday had been very hot, Wednesday was dry but cool; trains were busy all day and when an afternoon shuttle arrived at Tan-y-Bwlch with 83 passengers (seating capacity 50-at a pinch!) there was talk of records for the first time; in fact the bookings record for a day was lifted from 3108 to 3216. The following week got an increase percentage firmly established again, and it is confidently hoped that September will see the increase maintained.

Generally speaking it has been an excellent year for passenger comfort, with trains rarely filled to capacity and timekeeping extremely good. First class patronage has shown a marked decrease, but sales takings have been well up. Dduallt kiosk was the first unit to pass last year's total sales-as early as 11th August-and the total sales on the Railway had passed last year's figure by the end of August.

On the evening of 1st July there was a double event: *Linda* crossed Rhoslyn bridge for the first time on a trial run in which most of the staff participated, and the leading coach of the train was new tourist car No. 37 on its first trial trip to Dduallt. *Blanche* also had a trial run as far as the approach to Barn cutting on 18th July, to be followed by *Linda* two days later when the President of the Lands Tribunal visited the line. On 24th August a special was run at the unusual hour of 8.45 from Portmadoc for the Cambrian Archaeological Association; the train was hauled by *Earl of Merioneth* and its formation included representatives of most varieties of F.R. stock, pride of place going to the open bug-box No. 7, restored by Midland Group to its original condition and regrettably quite unsuited to the safety requirements of present-day passenger travel.

The face-lift given to Harbour station during the winter has been followed by similar treatment at Minffordd, where many pots of paint have been applied by the stationmaster to good effect. The amenities at Tan-y-Bwlch have taken a great stride forward, with the completion of the footbridge and its attendant footpath in time for its official

71.3   The long fourteen coach train seen on the left of the previous picture was recorded from *Linda* on Boston Lodge curve.

opening on 18th July. The ceremony was performed by representatives of John Players, who had arrived at Portmadoc Harbour in their steam launch *Nottingham Castle*.

The main activity in the erecting shop has been concentrated on construction of the new tourist coaches. No. 37 ran its first trial to Dduallt on 1st July and was ready for use when the Dduallt shuttle started running, whilst No. 38 is now well advanced. Although numbered in the same series as the W.H.R. bogie toastrack Hudsons, the term toastrack hardly does justice to the new vehicles. They are extremely solid, well-proportioned coaches which will not look out of place on main line (F.R.) trains, although the wooden slat seating and rather noisy, hard riding (to be improved with lighter primary and a form of secondary suspension) make them more suited to the shuttle service. They are in fact just what was intended: workmanlike and economical products, enabling the bug-boxes to be withdrawn for much-needed rebuilding.

The frame of No. 37 was the first of the Hudson frames overhauled by the White Rose Group. Bodywork is of sectional metal construction, mass-produced in jigs. The roof is timbered and the doors are the wooden half doors made redundant when the ex W.H.R. coaches 23 and 26 were rebuilt a few years ago. No. 37 is vacuum piped at present, but will be fully braked in due course. It has an external handbrake on the bottom end bogie. No. 38 is similar, but is being built on a frame of one of the original series of W.H.R. toastracks and is being equipped with full vacuum brake gear from the start.

The second stage of the Harbour resignalling came into use-again very early in the morning-on Wednesday, 28th July, and comprised the Up Advance signal and its associated electrical control equipment. Both signals, and the shunts, are lit electrically. The somersault signal fittings are to McKenzie & Holland's miniature design, but with new arms. On the wall of the goods shed is a Sykes miniature banner signal (for the guards).

At the other end of the line, a twenty-four foot upper quadrant came into use on 31st May as Dduallt Up Home signal, in readiness for the peak Diddy service, easing somewhat the rather difficult working here at busy times. Because of the sharp left-hand curve approaching the station, the sighting of this signal was not very good from an up train (marvellous from anywhere else!) so subsequently a mechanical repeater was added further out.

71.4   *Linda* was the first steam locomotive to cross Rhoslyn Bridge and was recorded in the company of new coach no. 37 on 1st July. The outcome of the Lands Tribunal's prolonged deliberations regarding compensation for the loss of the FR's direct route was still awaited.

Winter 1971

Good weather when it was needed most helped to boost the autumn figures, and it looks as if we shall end the year with a modest increase of between 2% and 3%. over 1970; it must be admitted that this is better than seemed likely in mid-August. Revenue from fares is up by 24%. and from sales by 30%. The trend throughout the year, apart from a disappointing period in late June and early July, has been in the direction of levelling out the peaks and troughs. Graduated fares have no doubt helped this desirable process, and will continue to do so as the advantages of off-peak travel become better known. Educational tours by large school parties are a growing source of useful traffic during fairly quiet times of the year.

There was a fine flourish at the end of October during the last week of week-day trains, when sunny weather and school half-term holidays yielded 2,491 passenger journeys, compared with 1,475 for the same week in 1970 - a 69% increase.

Since the first sod was cut on 2nd January 1965, deviation work has been largely confined to the spiral at Ddaullt. With the acquisition of the Massey Ferguson digger early in 1971 the trackbed progressed rapidly during the summer through Bluebell Site in the general direction of Tan-y-Grisiau, but pending finalisation of the route no work could be done after the point where the east side and west side routes diverge.

The breakthrough came early in October, when agreement was reached with the CEGB concerning the west side route and the deviationists were given the green light to start work on some portions of the route on CEGB land. The first site chosen was the ancient but solidly built dam (quite close to the northern portal of the old Moelwyn tunnel), which is reputed to have provided water power for the Moelwyn inclines. As will be seen from the diagram, the route passes through the reservoir and dam, the track level being a few feet lower than the top of the dam. Consequently, the first job at Dam Site is to remove a large portion from the centre of the dam so that the reservoir can be drained. To ensure that it stays drained a large culvert is being built through the breach, using rocks from the dam walls. At first it was thought that dismantling a man-made structure would provide welcome relief after the rigours of Barn Site and Dragon, but the size and weight of the blocks of stone in the dam have quickly encouraged a healthy regard for early nineteenth century dam builders. Incidentally, it is clear from the smooth faces found inside the dam that it was enlarged at least twice in its history, but excavations to date have not thrown any light on the actual operation of the water wheel, if indeed there was one.

A first sod ceremony was held on 16th October, when Mr. Golding, superintendent of Tan-y-Grisiau Power Station, removed the first lump of rock (and several more) from the top of the dam. The traditional golden spade was in attendance; less traditional were the golden toecaps on the Site Foreman's safety boots! The next sites to be started will be the approach cutting to the northern portal of the new tunnel and cuttings on either side of a gully about midway between the tunnel and the power station.

71.5 John Player's steam launch graced Portmadoc Harbour during July, but was seldom photographed in the presence of other forms of steam propulsion.

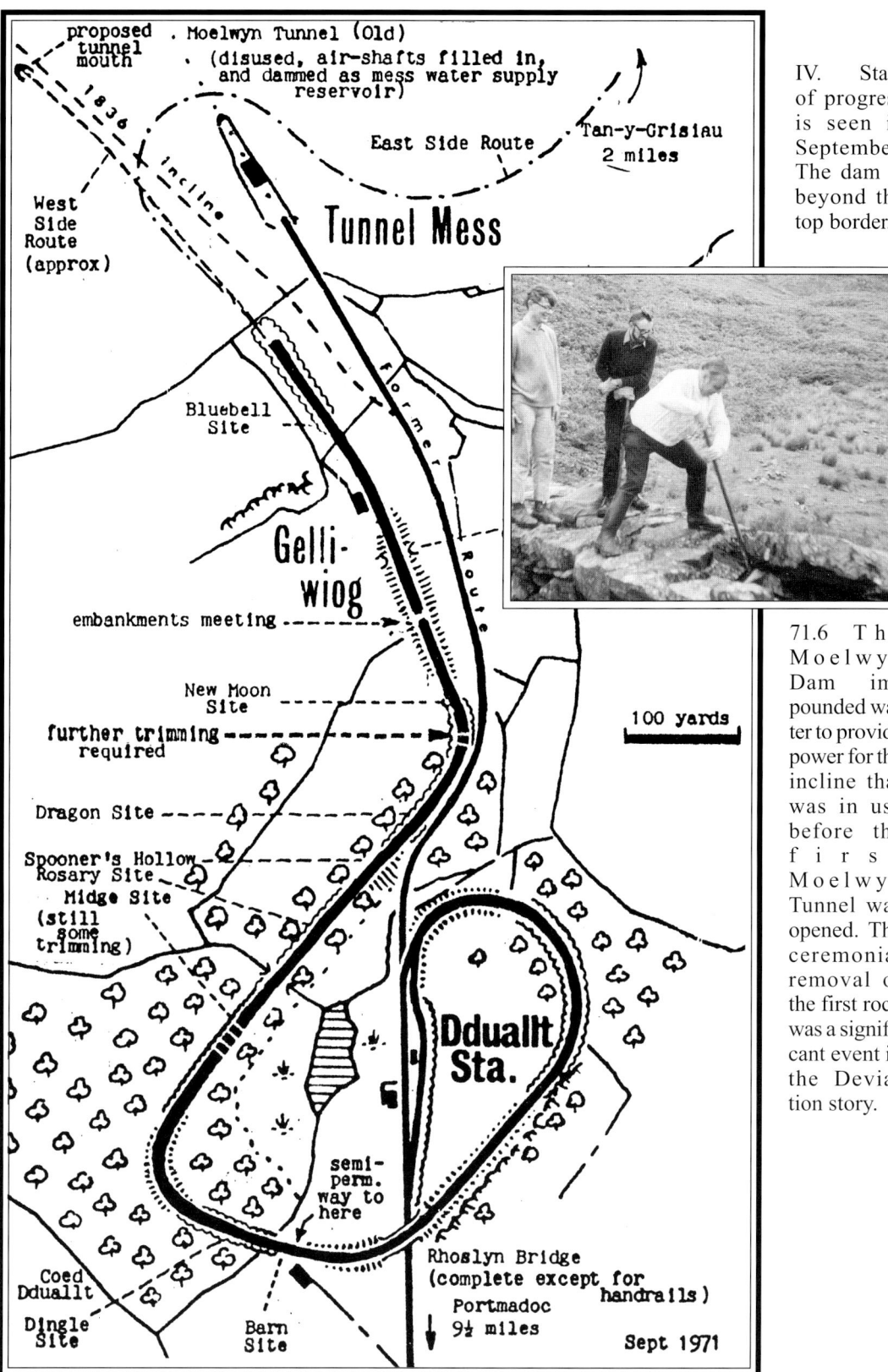

IV. State of progress is seen in September. The dam is beyond the top border.

71.6 The Moelwyn Dam impounded water to provide power for the incline that was in use before the first Moelwyn Tunnel was opened. The ceremonial removal of the first rock was a significant event in the Deviation story.

1972

Spring 1972

Locomotive mileages for 1971

Locomotive	1971	Total under present administration
Prince	nil	40,287
Earl of Merioneth	1,577	45,006
Merddin Emrys	5,932	18,007
Linda	8,047	38,447
Blanche	7,970	39,885
Mountaineer	2,331	14,209
Moelwyn	2,182	24,982
Upnor Castle	1,724	3,256
Tyke	nil	180
Alistair	725	3,171
Mary Ann	2,846	9,842
Wickham trolley	nil	10,187

The cladding of *Earl of Merioneth's* new boiler has been fitted and painted. New frames and boiler cradles are complete and design work is in hand for the tanks. A new extended front end unit for *Blanche* has been fabricated and welded to the frame; construction of the pony truck is progressing. The new firebox and boilerwork is in the hands of Midland Rolling & Haulage Company, Birmingham.

The building department have been making improvements to the facilities at Harbour Station, primarily with the installation of additional storage room above the booking hall. The inspection pit under No. 3 road has been completed and awaits the reinstatement of the track. Interior work at Tan-y-Bwlch signal box has reached an advanced stage; decorating will be completed after all the S & T equipment has been installed. Some wet weather work has been done in the Blacksmith's shop at Boston Lodge as part of the long term development programme.

An order has been placed with Edmund Crow, commercial bodybuilder, of Cleator Moor, Cumberland, to supply the bodywork and underframe of a prototype aluminium-bodied coach. Boston Lodge will be providing the bogies and associated running gear and the coach is scheduled to be in service before the start of the peak season. It will be a few inches longer than the present standard design, measuring 35ft. 9in. overall, and will be a somewhat different sort of vehicle from those which Edmund Crow has been producing in large numbers for the Ravenglass & Eskdale Railway.

In March the PW Department were involved, in conjunction with contractors, in pressure-grouting four underbridges (Gwyndy, Ty Fry, Rhiw Goch and Coed-y-Bleiddiau); yet another of the expensive chores which have been put off for decades but which cannot be overlooked indefinitely as the Railway continues to expand. For the future programme there's a section of straight track on Cei Mawr which must have attention soon and any amount of ballasting and tamping, particularly between Tan-y-Bwlch and Coed-y-Bleiddiau.

The new year on the Deviation got off to a prompt and promising start; on Saturday, 1st January, the Massey-Ferguson digger was driven cautiously from its over-Christmas parking lot at Tan-y-Grisiau power station to the vicinity of Dam Site, following the old route of the Railway for most of the way. Unexpectedly, that very day the power station started operating after about seven months' inactivity; the driver looked back to see his tracks covered by the rising tide and thanked his lucky stars he hadn't stopped for a second helping of porridge! Initial digging efforts have not been without their exciting moments, due to the prevalence of boggy peat, but large supplies of firewood sleepers acquired from the PW Dept. and carried laboriously over the hill from tunnel mess have helped to keep the machine on an even keel. Floundering in the boggy morass, into which the tunnel approach cutting will be cut, it is difficult to credit that in a few months' time the same site will involve the drilling of 20ft. blast holes in solid granite.

72.1 Pressure grouting of under-line structures involved forcing a cement mixture into the gaps in the stonework, using compressed air. The task was undertaken by a specialist contractor.

Summer 1972

Traffic Manager Alan Heywood has been frequently reminded that as soon as he drew attention last summer to the Railway's consistent 10% annual increase in traffic the 10% started to evaporate. He assures his correspondents that he has his beady little eye on the situation and is well satisfied with this year's results to date. Up to the start of Spring Bank Holiday week traffic was 8% up on the same period in 1971, in spite of the very wet Easter which brought a 10% reduction over this most remunerative part of the period. Spring Bank Holiday week was consistently busy, notwithstanding the intermittently dismal weather, and brought 26,808 passenger journeys - 1,200 more than in 1971 (which proved to be the second busiest week of the year). Tuesday (30th May) was the busiest day, with 2,733 bookings; the sales total for the week was only fractionally short of a record.

An intensive campaign, in conjunction with Quarry Tours, to promote schools traffic is having good results, and party bookings up to 8th July are exceptionally heavy. On 17th May 350 schoolchildren from Caernarvon were carried on a special train, hauled by *Merddin Emrys,* and on the same day *Mountaineer* took eight coaches on the 15.15. The day's total of 825 bookings was a record for this time of year.

Rail stocks have recently been augmented by the purchase of 1,900 track-yards of 75 lb./yard flat bottom rail, with turnouts, which became available when Tilbury power station sidings were relaid with heavier materials. The consignment, totalling about 150 tons, arrived at Minffordd yard on 30th May on four bogie bolster wagons and was unloaded and stacked with the help of a hired crane.

The latest outside job to arrive at Boston Lodge is easily the most notable so far: an 0-8-0 tender locomotive brought to this country from Germany by Mr. John Snell. Built by Orenstein & Koppel A.G., Berlin, in 1934, it was purchased from Deutsche Reichbahn (East German State Railways) on behalf of a group.

If Deviation progress is measured purely in terms of completed trackbed the winter's activity has not been very productive. In fact, the deviationists have been as busy as ever, moving shop, opening up new sites, exploring new techniques and generally preparing the way for intensive summer activity. The Company's lorry was at their disposal over Easter, and made four trips to Tan-y-Grisiau power station compound and beyond, loaded with a complete do-it-yourself railway building kit - compressor, tool shed, jubilee track, skips, tools and old sleepers.

There is plenty of evidence that the excavator has not been idle since arrival on site on 1st January. Outcrops of granite have been laid bare at "Tunnel North" site, where drilling and blasting is due to commence during June to open up the tunnel approach cutting. This is the first major professional contract on the Deviation.

72.2 Quarry Tours Ltd were establishing a successful operation at Llechwedd, but Oakeley had yet to follow. They had the attraction of this Emmett-style loco with ramshackle overhead wires, but the public was never to see it working and their site eventually closed.

Autumn 1972

The Traffic Manager's beady little eye was slightly bloodshot towards the end of July, but it had developed a healthy glint by early September. The weather pattern has followed roughly the same sort of trends as in 1971 and traffic figures have followed suit.

In spite of the record weeks there were no record days, traffic tending to be spread more evenly. This, together with the availability of extra seating capacity in tourist car No. 38 and a better spread of coach parties, greatly reduced the problems at Tan-y-Bwlch and virtually eliminated the need to run the Dduallt shuttle. There has been no marked change in hour-to-hour travelling habits, the early afternoon peak being as popular as ever in spite of increased publicity for off-peak and economy fares. The use of diesel power on the 9.40 and 17.45 departures has been widely announced, with no obvious drop in patronage but virtual elimination of complaints.

(top left)
72.3 Coach no. 116 was well advanced in May in Edmund Crow's Works at Cleaton Moor in Cumberland. It was a prototype to evaluate the practicalities of aluminium construction.

72.4 Features to be incorporated in no. 116 were inward opening doors to lobbies at each end, a first class compartment at one end, 33 third class seats in the open saloon, the roof insulated with fibreglass and lighting by 24v. fluorescent tubes.

On Sundays during the peak period Crosville ran a bus from Blaenau to Tan-y-Bwlch connecting with the principal service train from Llandudno. Tan-y-Bwlch stationmaster John Harrison noticed that the bus was doing little of use during what amounted to a 3-4 hour layover period, and suggested that it could earn revenue doing a return trip from Tan-y-Bwlch to the CEGB Stwlan Dam. After the Traffic Manager had spent the best part of a day on the telephone, the necessary arrangements were made and an afternoon excursion by rail and road to Stwlan was advertised on a board outside Harbour station. It ran fully booked for the rest of the season.

The regularity of a pleasantly smooth operating season was shattered on the Tuesday of the August Bank Holiday week. *Merddin Emrys*, running into Portmadoc sidings to pick up her first train, the 11.00 as usual, became derailed. It was immediately obvious that this was no ordinary derailment; one wheel was peculiarly out of line, and the cause was found to be a broken bottom end leading axle.

The "B" train set was blocked in No. 4 siding and spare coaches for "C" set in No. 5, but fortunately it was found that some of the shorter coaches (bug boxes, a tourist car and-with only a fraction of an inch to spare - No. 19) could be manhandled out of No. 4 and these were parked in the goods shed road with *Linda* to form the 11.45 train. Even with three engines available it was not easy to organise a two-train service without run-round facilities, but *Upnor Castle* and *Mountaineer* alternated on the "A" set, using the goods shed as an engine road, while *Linda* worked continuously on the heavy "C" set. The spare engine changed with *Linda* at Pen Cob to take the train to Port so that *Linda* could follow over to take the train up again.

Work on the new *Earl of Merioneth* has been largely at a standstill during the peak season, with two tanks virtually complete and two still to be constructed. In view of *Merddin's* broken axle there must obviously be some reprogramming as far as the Fairlies are concerned, with *Earl's* completion date put back considerably.

The body of the new 41-seater coach arrived in July after a long delay while the builders awaited windows. This, too, was obviously going to miss the summer peak traffic, and while its bogies were being prepared a start was made on bringing the bodywork up to Boston Lodge standards, some aspects of its workmanship leaving a lot to be desired.

Further improvements to buildings are in hand. The original loco shed latterly used for carriage storage, is the present preoccupation of the building department. The unsightly part of the shed nearest the main road has been demolished and is being replaced with a longer but narrower structure. This will enable a roadway to be put in round the outside to give vehicles access, on special occasions, to the works yard. The third track will be extended through the end of the new building to the loading dock alongside Boston Lodge halt, used mainly for gas cylinders.

72.5 Genuine horse traffic returned in July when a Portmadoc resident, who did not relish the heavy road traffic on a visit to Minffordd, found the FR tariff cheaper than hiring a road vehicle. No. 9 van was used.

Winter 1972

The prototype aluminium-bodied corridor coach, No. 116, entered service at the end of October, exactly 100 years after the FR's first bogie coaches, Nos. 15 and 16. Passenger reaction is being gauged by means of a questionnaire and general first impressions seem to be very satisfactory, although the somewhat revolutionary (by British narrow gauge standards) ventilation and insulation system will have its real test in hot weather conditions while the general construction of the coach can only be said to have proved itself after decades of service. Its heating system-electrical storage heaters under the seats-is providing additional comfort and should be particularly welcome on the Christmas trains. A similar installation has been functioning in coach 105 for some time. As these heaters can be adjusted to give low heat as well as normal, they should help to reduce winter storage dampness problems.

As a result of discussions on the Convention special it has been decided to experiment with Non-Smoking compartments. This has been resisted for many years, on account of the difficulties that could arise at the busiest times, but with more people wanting non-smoking accommodation and over-crowding problems being eased over the last two years, it is felt that the idea can now be tried.

Although there can be no reduction in the amount of work being done between Porthmadog and Dduallt, the PW Dept. is, nevertheless, very conscious of the need for ever-increasing activity beyond Dduallt if the Railway is to be reopened to Blaenau in 1978 as planned. Programming is, of course, closely tied up with Deviation progress, but with the track-bed virtually complete as far as Dragon Site there is no reason why things should not get started during 1973. 1,000 jarrah sleepers have been ordered, for delivery as early in the summer as possible, and the acquisition of rail (either new 60 lb or second-hand 75 lb) is actively under consideration.

Once permanent track has been laid through to Dragon Site—or perhaps a little beyond-effort will be concentrated on the Tan-y-Grisiau to Glan-y-Pwll section until the Moelwyn tunnel is finished in 1975. (The section of deviation track-bed immediately west of the power station scheduled for completion in 1974 will have no rail access and may not be considered of sufficient length to justify the extra expense and trouble of using road transport for track materials and personnel.)

Apart from the pointwork at Dduallt and, maybe later, the unpleasantness of working in the tunnel, the track-laying on the deviation is straightforward work and initially is being entrusted to one or two members of the staff with, it is hoped, a good muster of volunteers. This year's commencing date will, of course, depend on availability of materials, but there is a good chance that PW volunteers arriving between Whitsun and September will spend at least a part of their stay on this work. To ensure minimum deterioration of rails and sleepers, it is proposed to complete the track to a high standard, with a reasonable bed of ballast. This means that regular ballast trains will be running from Minffordd often at odd times of the day-or night!

Much less straightforward is the mile of track between Tan-y-Grisiau and Glan-y-Pwll. This includes innumerable civil engineering problems: bridges, dozens of culverts, retaining walls, fences and drains, all requiring expert and labour-consuming attention either before or in conjunction with track work.

72.6   Van no. 9 had spent its working life on the Welshpool & Llanfair Railway and had been regauged and rebuilt by the Milton Keynes Group. It was provided with a through vacuum pipe. It is seen at Tan-y-Bwlch in the company of *Alistair*.

72.7   The prototype aluminium coach no. 116 was recorded as it entered traffic in October. It was mounted on standard bogies and was positioned adjacent to no. 16, which had been built for the FR 101 years earlier and was one of the first bogie coaches in regular use in Great Britain.

72.8   Featured is the replacement for the semi-derelict extension of the former locomotive shed, close to Boston Lodge Halt. The use of modern materials speeded construction.

72.9   Oil tankers were created from ex-road vehicles. As there was no road access to Boston Lodge, transfer of fuel oil from road to rail had to be made elsewhere, usually in Minffordd Yard.

1973

Spring 1973

Locomotive mileages for 1972

	1972	Total under present administration
Prince	nil	40,287
Earl of Merioneth	nil	45,006
Merddin Emrys	6,908	24,915
Linda	7,557	46,004
Blanche	274	40,159
Mountaineer	12,486	26,695
Moelwyn	2,624	27,606
Upnor Castle	2,924	6,180
Tyke	nil	180
Alistair	630	3,821
Mary Ann	1,861	11,703
Jane	708	1,410
Wickham Trolley	11	10,198

A good honest digging site is now well established in the blasted granite of tunnel north approach cutting, and the track formation now leads across the bed of the old reservoir, through the dam (with temporary decking over the major culvert at this point) and is extending every week-end in the general direction of New site. The embankment is a fairly shallow one for most of the way, on a gently sloping hillside, and progress should be rapid even though the loaded skips have to be pushed uphill an ever-increasing distance. Some clearance of turf has to be done ahead of the embankment as it creeps forward and there are three culverts (two of 2 ft diameter and one of 4 ft) to be installed *en route*.

At the south end of the tunnel efforts have been concentrated on providing firm road access to the site via the old inclines. The excavator will shortly be used to clear overburden and expose the rock on the southern approach cutting site, so that the contractor can get his drilling and blasting done.

73.1 The site between the erecting shop and the old quarry face was cleared early in the year to permit extension of the building.

73.2 BR removed its connection at Minffordd early in 1973; the last locomotive to arrive by rail was John Snell's ex-German 0-8-0 for repair at Boston Lodge.

Summer 1973
The removal of Porthmadog coaling stage in March signified the Railway's total commitment to oil firing for the foreseeable future, and the emergence of *Merddin Emrys* from the works for passenger train duties on 24th April quickly vindicated the confidence shown in the Fairlie's conversion. *Merddin* walked away with a test train and then a twelve-coach service train, and a few days later handled the late-evening twelve-coacher on AGM day. From the start the main problem has been to keep the rate of steam production *down* to the most economical level, particularly on the downhill run.

The wide open spaces of Minffordd yard offer great scope for development and the recent closure and removal of the standard-gauge sidings marks another stage in the modernisation of the yard. The theme for the future is, of course, road/rail (n.g.) transhipment, and the road approach to the yard and especially to the ballast chutes has already been vastly improved. In the longer term it is planned to build a new road from the weigh-house corner to the new carriage sheds, thus providing a circular route through the yard and alleviating the present problems of turning cumbersome lorries in very restricted spaces. The surplus spoil from the road works will be used to fill in the sunken areas vacated by the standard-gauge tracks, and eventually the whole yard will be on one level with the exception of the siding under the chutes (which no doubt will continue to be known as the coal road for many

---

73.3 By May, temporary way had passed through the breach in the dam, visible in the background. This is a northward view from near the site of the proposed tunnel. At about this time, the first batch of brand new rail arrived on the revived FR; it was three miles in length.

years) and its spur. The lifting capacity of the gantry and the ex-GWR crane (now standing on a very short piece of track) will be augmented by a mobile crane.

The goods shed was gutted last autumn and is now ready to receive a concrete floor to facilitate PW work, such as the assembly of turnouts and the pre-drilling of sleepers.

Early in the year the top ground frame at Dduallt was brought into use, controlling the main line turnout to Moelwyn Mess siding and its associated single-tongue trap. At the bottom end of the station the shunting disc signals had to be modified to improve sighting from incoming trains; the new variation incorporates an ex-L & SW short lattice post supporting a small cantilevered platform carrying the signals. The lever interlocking at Dduallt was among various items of equipment tested and found satisfactory by an Inspecting Officer on 14th April.

Tunnel North approach cutting continues to grow, as does the embankment leading from it through the old reservoir towards New site. Preparatory work at Tunnel South got well and truly bogged down in the peat, but additional drainage measures have been put in hand and progress should be more rapid as the site dries out. A digging site has already been established at the shallow end, and after top-soil removal the contractor will be drilling and blasting the main part of the cutting. This site is earmarked for "Humpty Dumpty"-the Atlas Copco mine loader purchased in derelict condition from the disposal sale at Dorothea Quarry, Nantlle, in 1970, and now restored to working order.

73.4 A special cradle had to be constructed to convey a new water tank from Boston Lodge to Harbour station. The assembly is standing outside the pre-1939 locomotive running shed.

73.5   A snap from the managerial sitting room window features *Merddin Emrys* with an unusual 13-coach train. The historic Britannia Foundry buildings would soon vanish.

73.6   Rhoslyn bridge is in the background as *Merddin Emrys* stops with a special train conveying councillors to inspect the southern part of the Deviation on 7th July.

Autumn 1973

The construction of an entirely new concept of underframe is well advanced for use, in this particular instance, to mount an additional 2,000 gallon fuel tank for locomotive use and also to prove the design, both in construction and performance, in service, with a view to its use under any passenger cars that may be constructed in the future. As a tank car, this vehicle will be run on imported ex-Polish State Railways 60cm plate-framed bogies salvaged from snow ploughs and suitably modified with standard FR drawgear and centres. A further consignment of these and diamond-framed bogies is on order from the same source and should greatly ease the current shortage of bogies which has been hindering the planning of similar projects.

Flat bottom rails have also become very much a part of the lives of the works staff in recent months. Apart from providing crane drivers and slingers at Minffordd yard to off load new rails ex-Workington and sort and load rails bound for Dduallt, the works have completed the dismantling, modification to reduce the flange gaps, etc., and re-assembly of four former standard gauge turnouts, ex-Tilbury, and work on a further batch is in hand to meet PW requirements for the coming winter.

On Sunday, 24th June, Mountaineer pulled away from Minffordd with a load of rails, sleepers and ballast. On arrival at Dduallt the Deviation excavator dragged the rails forward into Barn cutting, and the laying of permanent track on the Deviation started. Initially, work proceeded forwards from a junction outside the Barn with the old bull-head semi-permanent track, through Barn cutting, round the sharp curve at Dingle and on to the straight at Midge. By the end of July this section had been laid and packed roughly level.

These materials were conveyed to Dduallt in steam-hauled trains, leaving Minffordd at 18.30. The loco would run round at Dduallt and propel the train to the required position. Unloading would take place next day and the empties would be gravitated to Minffordd in the evening and positioned for reloading. By 8th August 12 trains had run, conveying 500 tons of ballast and 50 tons of rail, as well as sleepers, fence stakes and many miscellaneous loads. After that, a weekly ballast train sufficed, with the wagons returning to Minffordd loaded with bull-head materials.

On the Tan-y-Grisiau—Blaenau section, most of the activity so far has taken the form of surveying, programming and report writing. The first actual working party descended on Glan-y-Pwll from London on 18-19th August and commenced the clearance of rubbish from the old loco shed and the area outside.

73.7   One of the many major tasks to be undertaken on the upper part of the route was the replacement of the bridge over the Afon Barlwyd at Glan-y-Pwll. It had carried double track.

Winter 1973

The year 1973 has been one of expansion at the works, with the accent on buildings and plant. The aim is to enable locomotive overhauls and rolling stock construction and repairs to be carried out with greater efficiency and independence in the future, but in the meantime there has to be a period in which only a modest programme of mainly routine maintenance can be pursued.

By the end of November the cladding of the new erecting shop extension was virtually complete and the floor had been concreted. Although incomplete at the eastern end, the building was able to receive its first occupant - the torso of the new *Earl of Merioneth*. Work has commenced on the former bottom-end bogie from *Merddin Emrys*-the one that received damage as a result of the axle failure in August 1972. The opportunity is being taken to manufacture many new parts, sometimes to an improved design, such as intermediate valve spindles and motion plates, slidebars and crossheads. Similarly the ballast weight at the rear of the bogie, which is in fact loose, will be redesigned to incorporate such equipment as the steam brake cylinder. A new leading axle will be made and fitted, along with new driving wheel crankpins, to prove that Boston Lodge's machining capacity is equal to this class of work.

In Glan-y-Mor, the shell of the new Atcost joiners' and paintshop building is complete and cladding is in hand.

Following the successful installation of 75 lb f/b turnouts at each end of Rhiw Goch loop, the relaying of Tan-y-Bwlch West junction (i.e. the two at the bottom end of the station) was started in mid-November and completed by the end of the month. The two 75 lb turnouts were constructed on top of the siding, where they were out of everybody's way and could be worked on intermittently, and then dragged and slewed into position after the old turnouts had been lifted and the beds levelled.

Work on the permanent track at Dduallt ceased for the year in mid-September and is unlikely to recommence before June 1974. Some weekend parties have been in evidence at Blaenau during the autumn, lifting what remained of the old track on either side of Glan-y-Pwll level crossing and laying a siding into the old loco shed. As the shed will be used to house a small Simplex now being overhauled by the North Staffs Group, a start has been made on making the shed vandal-proof.

After ten years and something like 10,000 bed-nights, we have vacated Dduallt Mess. In future, Campbell's Platform will be just that; it will no longer be "Hairy's Halt" or "Lemon's Leap" and the Sunday evening trains will pass it by without having to stop and fill their guard's vans with diggers and luggage returning to the Metropolis. To Colonel and Mrs Campbell we express our sincere thanks for putting up with us for so long. Most of the furniture and fittings have been taken to our new quarters in Tan-y-Grisiau.

The FR is not officially restricted to a three-day week, as railways and light railways are specifically exempt, but nevertheless every effort has been made to economise. Boston Lodge has been virtually closing down and not using any electricity on Mondays and Tuesdays, and has been observing strict daytime hours on other days.

73.8   The derelict locomotive shed at Glan-y-Pwll is seen shortly before work started on establishing an engineering centre, from which work in the upper section could be organised.

1974

Spring 1974

Locomotive mileages for 1973

	1973	Total under present administration
Prince	nil	40,287
Earl of Merioneth	nil	45,006
Merddin Emrys	5,253	30,168
Linda	5,005	51,009
Blanche	11,432	51,591
Mountaineer	7,405	34,100
Moelwyn	2,398	30,004
Upnor Castle	2,109	8,289
Tyke	nil	180
Alistair	880	4,701
Mary Ann	547	12,250
Jane	1,385	2,795
Wickham Trolley	14	10,212

Although less susceptible to fuel and power restrictions than other departments, the PW gang have had their full share of discomfort and frustrations. The rain that fell on all but two days between Christmas and the start of the 1974 passenger service, the gremlins that tampered relentlessly with every bit of electrical equipment the department possesses, and difficulties in obtaining supplies of ballast due to short working and breakdowns at the quarries, all combined to slow down many of the processes that go to make up a successful winter's work.

100 tons of new 60lb. rail was delivered to Minffordd in late February/early March and it is proposed that the next delivery will be consigned to Glan-y-pwll.

The long-too-long-push from Tunnel North cutting to the tipping end of the embankment is being mechanised at last, and the proving trials of the motorised skip are awaited with keen interest. In the meantime, a 2ft diameter culvert has to be installed before the embankment can continue to extend towards its eventual link-up with New Site. Much rock still has to be removed from the cutting, but thanks to the Smalley visible progress is made every week-end.

Progress at Tunnel South has been hampered by the wet weather and there is still a vast amount of peat to be removed to permit the rock to be drilled and blasted. Whatever the weather, waders have to be worn at this site and workers are compulsorily hosed down before being allowed to enter the mess.

74.1 The foundations for the extension of the Harbour station building towards the goods shed were started in February. The lower window then served the Ladies Room. Not only were there major alterations to the buildings, but the name of the town changed from Portmadoc to Porthmadog.

74.2 The erection of the steelwork for the future buffet area and offices began in March. The roof space in the goods shed (right) eventually became an uncomfortable repository for the FR archives.

74.3 The tank seen cradled on page 31 was raised to its resting place at the southern end of the line in March. The new building framework is complete in the background.

Summer 1974

The fuel crisis that had us all so worried only a few months ago does not seem to be having any repercussions as far as 1974 traffic figures are concerned; results in fact are remarkably consistent with last year's figures. The Spring Bank Holiday period, which was a little disappointing last year, gave the 1974 results a welcome boost, and we ended May about 5%. up.

A BR railtour which brought 537 passengers from Sheffield on 23rd March is believed to have been the biggest rail-borne party to visit the FR and was particularly valuable at this quiet time of year. Schools party traffic is also continuing to show an increase. Sales figures are still expanding more quickly than traffic, even allowing for inflation, with the buffet cars and Tan-y-Bwlch cafe making particularly promising starts to the season.

Needless to say, the increasing cash receipts are only going a small way towards subsidising the 150% increase in the cost of oil since last summer. The oil consumed by *Linda or Blanche* taking an average train to Dduallt and back costs just under £10 instead of about £4. As *Upnor Castle* can do the round trip with a light train on under £1-worth of the same fuel, the diesel has been appearing regularly on the first train out of Porthmadog. For a period all passengers travelling behind *Upnor Castle* were handed a notice reading as follows:

All Festiniog Railway locomotives (even the steam ones) use oil as a fuel and, as everybody knows, the cost of oil has risen dramatically in the last few months. The present fares have *not* been increased to cover this new expense.

In an attempt to avoid such a fare increase the Company is using the more economical diesel locomotives on a few of the quieter trains. Inevitably this has resulted in a small number of complaints from steam enthusiasts.

74.4   The massive manual task of laying the permanent way on the Deviation was recorded in July, near Dragon Site. Several power tools were to help speed the work.

Autumn 1974

The inclusive tour to Llechwedd Caverns has done particularly well. Crosville have been able to supply two vehicles at peak times this year, which has doubled the potential. The snag is that it produces a large unbalanced party down from Tan-y-Bwlch at 16.11-the least desirable part of the afternoon as far as that journey is concerned.

The revised fare structure has predictably helped to boost off-peak travel; on 13th August the 17.45 up had eight well-filled coaches. This has taxed Boston Lodge's rostering system at times, with *Upnor Castle* having to be substituted by a more powerful engine on several occasions at short notice.

On 15th July the first train of the day was unfortunate enough to be involved in an incident with a tree fallen across the line in the woods. Although the engine, *Mountaineer*, hit the tree, the driver had managed to bring the train virtually to a halt and fortunately damage was confined to one of the smokebox door handles and the telegraph wires. The next two up trains were combined at Penrhyn and without too much delay the service returned to normal. Another incident, on 14th August, also involved the first up train of the day, when *Upnor Castle* and the first coach (empty) were derailed on the catch points at the top end of Minffordd station. After some delay subsequent trains were able to use the loop line while re-railing and track repairs were carried out.

Evening works trains ran from Minffordd to Dduallt and back on about a dozen occasions during August, loading this year being restricted to 70 tons gross to lessen the risk of delaying passenger services. With complicated shunts at Dduallt and other points, it was often 11.00 p.m. before the day's operating could be said to be completed.

Events at Boston Lodge are inevitably overshadowed by the fact that the first new locomotive built there for over 90 years (and the first new Fairlie in the world for over 60) is now approaching the stage where fittings and details are added to a basically complete locomotive. The main body is, of course, completely new, but even the

---

74.5 *Palmerston* was loaded onto the FR's lorry in Minffordd Yard on 20th July. It was destined for Derby, having been purchased by a group of people who had the long-term aim of reviving the ruin. Few others then believed that it would steam again on the FR.

motor bogies, nominally existing ones being re-used, have many improvements and new parts. The now recognisable Fairlie rightly occupies the central position in the spacious new erecting shop.

Work has begun on a new 35 ft. "tourist" carriage for service in 1975 and the fleet of oil fuel tank wagons has been improved by the fitting of electric pumps, a detail for which it is hoped volunteer firemen are sufficiently grateful. Breakdown van 99 is having some palliative treatment pending the implementation of a project to provide improved facilities.

The "Bimmelbahn" 0-8-0 from East Germany, owned by a group headed by John Snell, has had little attention since it arrived at Boston Lodge for repair in 1972, apart from a smart red paint job applied by the owners. It may be said that this delay is not their wish, but rather a reflection of the ever increasing demands made on the works by the expanding railway, leaving little time over for specialised repair work on outside locomotives.

Work has been in progress at Rhiw Goch through the summer, and installation of the lever frame was sufficiently advanced to permit erection of the signal box by the North Staffs Group on 7-8th September. Conditions could not have been worse in such an exposed location; a lady volunteer saved an awkward situation by preventing a roof support from crashing to the ground-with her head-but the job was completed and installation of the fittings and electrical gear can proceed.

In spite of all the problems, Tunnel South is beginning to take shape and the embankment is creeping out towards Two Trees. This embankment is to be of particularly wide formation; firstly because of the vast surplus of rock expected to be available and secondly because it is hoped that a permanent siding or loop can be provided as well as additional temporary trackwork which will be needed in connection with the tunnel boring. The embankment will probably be of only single line width initially, so that the permanent track can be extended into the site as quickly as possible.

74.6 *Upnor Castle* and coach 17 on the ballast at Minffordd on 14th August was not widely publicised. Even the FR Magazine did not have a picture of it.

74.7   Extension of the railway brought the need for a passing loop in the vicinity of Penrhyn. The track and signal box base at Rhiw Goch were completed by the Summer.

74.8   The inelegant but economical signal box at Rhiw Goch was bolted together in August. One siding was provided, but no platforms. Staff arrive on the first train of the day.

Winter 1974

One important change from present practice is that Boston Lodge, Plas, Coed-y-Bleiddiau and Campbell's Platform will receive a stopping train only once every two hours, though all trains will continue to call when required for staff purposes only.

Yet another innovation for 1975 will be the introduction of a shuttle service between Dduallt and Gelliwiog. This will be operated by a special diesel-hauled push and pull train, and will run as required during the summer months. Passengers will not be able to alight at Gelliwiog.

The new coach for the shuttle service (will it be the first-ever two-foot gauge auto-control-trailer?) is planned also to be the first FR passenger coach on Polish bogies. A pair of the diamond-framed variety has been allocated.

Drilling and blasting has at last started at Tan-y-Grisiau station. The large mass of rock alongside the site of the old station has to be cut into, to provide a greatly enlarged, curving station area some three feet higher than the old formation level. This increased height will run out in the cutting above the station. At the top end of the station site the roof of an existing public subway is being raised and at the bottom end a long 2ft.-diameter culvert has to be installed. This site is only intended for hand working at present, and then only when Tunnel South is fully manned.

Further round the route, some trial digging will be done shortly where the line will be crossing the Afon Cwmorthin in the area behind the power station reception centre. This will be to ascertain the form of construction required for the bridge abutments. The contract work close to the power station is not being progressed at present, simply because all available funds are required for the tunnel. The long, straightforward section between that area and the end of the embankment leading from Tunnel North may be done as a spare-time job by a friendly Blaenau contractor, but if he doesn't have any spare time it will have to be tackled by the Massey as soon as it can be spared from other work.

74.9 The new buildings at Harbour station were well advanced when photographed in November, along with the Simplex and coach 11.

1975

Spring 1975

Your waste oil can help to keep FR wheels turning. Please deliver in cans to Boston Lodge Works, you can take away the empties, or similar ones, for refilling. Anyone who can put the Railway in touch with sources of bulk waste oil, say 500 gallons or more, should get in touch with the Works Manager or General Manager, please. The economics of transporting waste oil have to be considered very carefully, but there is great scope for easing our fuel bill in this way.

The timetable from 17th May to 21st September has been completely re-cast. Throughout this period some trains will not stop at the halts.

Rhiw Goch passing loop is scheduled to commence daily use on 17th May and to handle crossings until 21st September. From 17th to 25th May, 31st May to 6th July and 30th August to 21st September, all timetabled crossings will take place there. There is no public access to Rhiw Goch and passengers will not be able to alight from or board trains there.

The Dduallt-Gelliwiog shuttle service will commence on 17th May (or as soon after that date as possible) and run according to demand. It will be a "paytrain" service, with no through bookings from other stations and no free travel or concessionary tickets of any sort. Passengers will not be able to alight from or board trains at Gelliwiog.

Locomotive mileages for 1974

	1974	Total under present administration
Prince	nil	40,287
Earl of Merioneth	nil	45,006
Merddin Emrys	4,762	34,930
Linda	8,088	59,097
Blanche	10,250	61,841
Mountaineer	4,163	38,263
Moelwyn	3,311	33,315
Upnor Castle	3,004	11,893
Tyke	nil	180
Alistair	863	5,564
Mary Ann	238	12,488
Jane	1,398	4,193
Diana	167	167
Wickham Trolley	nil	10,212
Mines Loco	2	2

The decision has been made to construct the new Moelwyn tunnel by direct labour, but confirmation is still awaited that funds will be available to enable work to start on the scheduled date - 1st September.

In the meantime, a vast amount of rock still has to be moved from the Tunnel South cutting. The Smalley took up residence there before Christmas, and after tidying up the floor of the upper level, was converted to face-shovel format for a concentrated attack on the low level. By the end of January, drilling and blasting to formation level was well in hand and week-end parties were getting into the habit of shifting rock at the rate of 50-100 skip-loads per day, many of the skips being taken to Gelliwiog by *Jane* in rakes of five.

75.1 New rails were lying ready in May, south of Glan-y-Pwll. The top end had good bullhead rail but some poor infrastructure. However there were political reasons for starting laying rails here.

Summer 1975

The new Deviation shuttle set emerged from the works in primer finish on trial towards the end of May. New is certainly the adjective to describe it. Ex-coal-mining diesel *Moel Hebog* is in appearance as might be expected, but the coach, or rather car, which accompanies it is more like the last word from Swiss Wagonsfabrik Schliereren in modernising a mountain railway. It is a long open vehicle, fabricated from steel plate and box sections, having domed ends to the roof. Weather protection in the form of end windows is given to the driving position, although perhaps this term is strictly incorrect because, for the time being, the equipage can be slowed or stopped from the car but not actually driven.

At Blaenau, 600 yards of the old track has be lifted and stacked. The new materials are ready at Glan-y-Pwll (except the rails, which are laid out along the trackbed) and a good number of sleepers have been pre-drilled, so that track laying can start in earnest during June if sufficient volunteers are available. As in 1974, the tendency will be for weekend working parties to work at Blaenau and the smaller numbers of weekday volunteers to concentrate on the Dduallt area, but by August it is expected that much of the weekday work will be at Blaenau as well.

If yardage (or metre-age) of roughly completed trackbed were the sole criterion, the Deviation has been leaping forward in spectacular fashion. Of course, the unavoidable high cost of much of the remaining work is a sobering influence, but there is still good cause for satisfaction over recent progress.

Confirmation that the Wales Tourist Board would assist the tunnel boring with a 49% grant and that work would definitely start on 1st September was a great boost to morale. With record numbers of workers responding to appeals, the Smalley simply ploughed into Tunnel South Cutting, and by Spring Bank Holiday the basic mucking out was finished.

75.2   The FR's long history of innovation and technical development had another chapter added in May, when the push-pull coach no.110 first saw the light of day. It had a semi-stressed skin and a centre spine underframe.

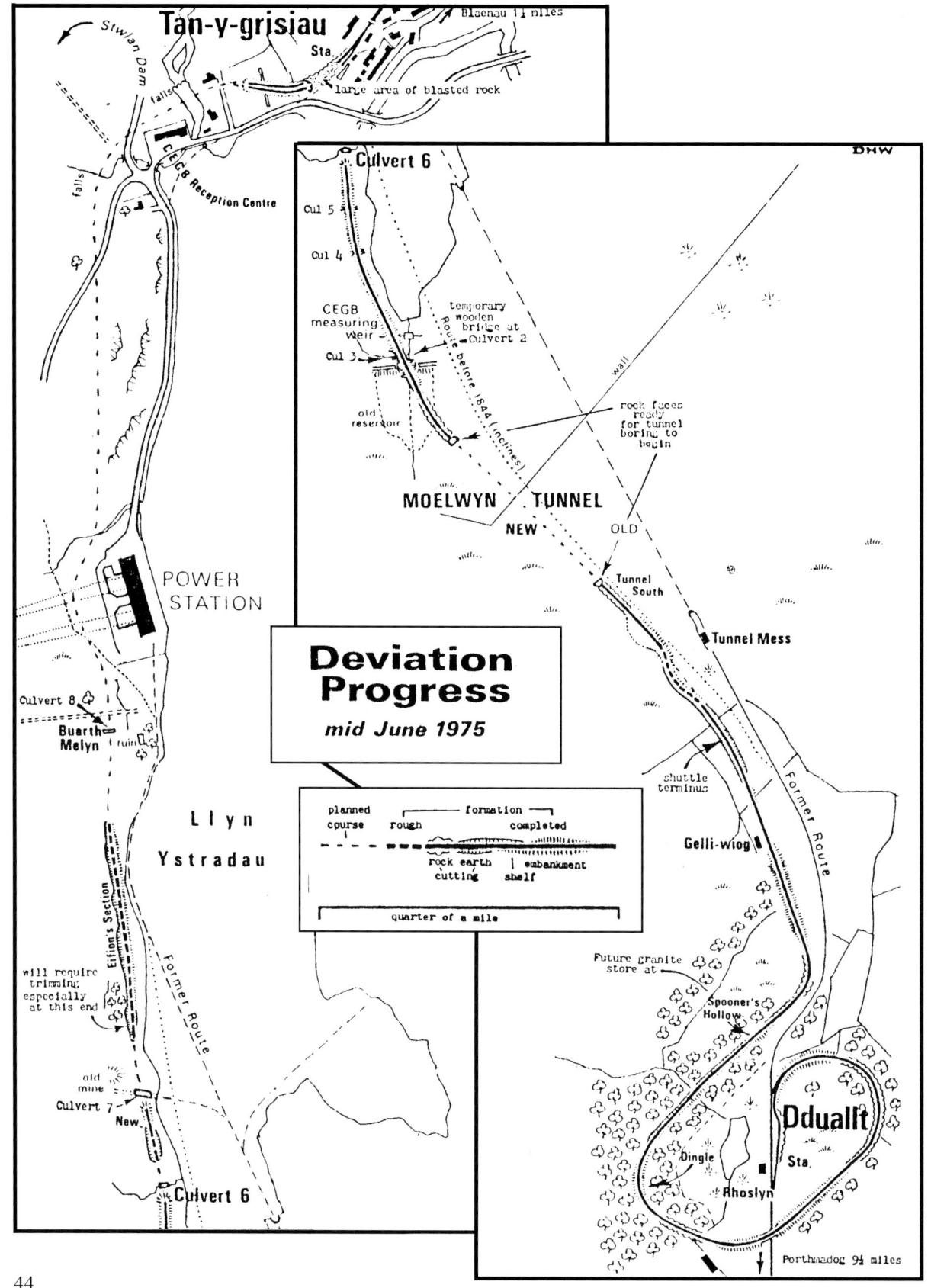

75.3 The new route on the west side of Llyn Ystradau was plain to see in June. In the foreground is the alignment of the pre-1842 incline, exposed recently by construction vehicles.

Autumn 1975

The Gelliwiog shuttle loco and coach spent most of June in the works, returning to service at the beginning of July in a considerably improved and more reliable condition. After various experiments it was found expedient for the loco and coach to travel to Dduallt in the formation of the first train up, and to return to Boston Lodge under its own power at about 17.30 from Dduallt. The shuttle service has proved reasonably successful, carrying over 10,000 people up to August Bank Holiday, but support varies from day to day and seems to depend more than anything else on the persuasive powers of the main train guards to encourage their passengers to relinquish their seats on arrival at Dduallt; this is particularly difficult towards the end of the afternoon when people are thinking more about their evening meal.

With the Gelliwiog shuttle safely running on continuously fenced track, any thoughts that the department would have a fairly leisurely summer were dispelled on 30th June by the announcement that *Princess Margaret's* train would run to Tunnel South on 24th July. This gave about three weeks in which to lay 1,000 ft. of permanent track onwards from Gelliwiog over track-bed which even the deviationists admitted as hardly ready. Fortunately

---

75.4 *Moel Hebog* appeared at the top end of Dduallt with the push-pull coach in July; it had entered service on 26th May and was the FR's first all-steel clad coach, no. 110.

there was a plentiful supply of labour from the Inter-Schools Christian Fellowship parties from the Moelwyn Mess, who were only too pleased to try their hand at track laying as an alternative to a daily trek to Tan-y-Grisiau to shift rock, and they proved capable platelayers, though the department's shortage of supervisory staff presented problems from time to time.

Preparations for the tunnel work have gone smoothly enough and most of the 1,001 items of equipment had arrived on site by the end of August, a notable exception being a second-hand battery electric locomotive being put into good working order by Mr. Alan Keef prior to delivery, and means of charging same which awaits provision of mains electricity. Temporary charging facilities may have to be used from the top siding at Tan-y-Bwlch.

The tunnel boring got under way in unspectacular fashion at the beginning of September, the first few weeks being devoted to the tricky work of shoring up a temporary portal. The operation of the new compressed-air-driven Atlas Copco loader is of particular interest. It is hoped the next *Magazine* will not only record good progress but also introduce the men and methods involved in this somewhat unusual (for the 1970's) undertaking.

75.5   The Royal Train was given a trial run to the temporary platform at Tunnel South on 23rd July. The Tunnel Mess is in the left background.

Winter 1975
On the Dduallt-Gelliwiog service, there were 15,000 passengers (i.e. 30,000 journeys). We got considerably better at "selling" this service towards the end of the season, and so hope that we can improve on this next year. Contrary to a recent suggestion in the *Magazine*, it is not so much the attitude of the shuttle guard which sells the service as that of the main train guards; they can do a lot to help by pushing leaflets and talking to passengers in the corridor stock.

Some experiments were conducted during the summer propelling a main-line train. The purpose behind the trials was to confirm that there are no problems in propelling entire rakes of coupled stock at train speeds and through all normal reverse curves. Coach No. 30 is at present in the works having a throttle control fitted to enable

---

75.6   An unexpected and unwanted problem arose in November when rocks that had supported the FR successfully for about 140 years fell into the kitchen of Penlan Cottage, above Tanygrisiau.

the shuttle loco to be driven by the "motorman", on the Gelliwiog service. Last summer the motorman only had control of brakes and horn. Finishing off work on seats and body also continues, including fitting of doors and droplight windows.

Work has proceeded during the autumn on the completion of Glan-y-Mor carriage shed, the work being entrusted to regular parties of volunteers. The walls are of breeze blocks up to a height of about 6 ft. and with large windows from there up to the eaves. On the seaward side the walls are up and the window frames in position, and work has started on the works side. There will also be a couple of rooms in a lean-to building outside the corner of the new shed nearest to the erecting shop, one of which will probably house a small machine shop.

75.7 New rails and sleepers were in position for a great distance above Tanygrisiau, years before they would support passengers. The cottage with the white end is the one damaged by the rockfall seen in the previous picture. Some of the new track had to be removed.

1976

Spring 1976

Locomotive mileages for 1975

Locomotive	1975	Total under present administration
Prince	nil	40,287
Earl of Merioneth	nil	45,006
Merddin Emrys	3,602	38,532
Linda	8,388	67,485
Blanche	11,070	72,911
Mountaineer	5,122	43,385
Moelwyn	3,535	36,850
Upnor Castle	2,684	14,577
Moel Hebog	2,346	2,348
Mary Ann	812	13,300
Tyke	nil	180
Alistair	461	6,025
Jane	2,201	6,394
Diana	494	661
Andrew	168	168
Wickham Trolley	nil	10,212
BEV	518	518

Upnor Castle has had some attention and is now fitted for auto-working; this would permit its use as a standby on the Gelliwiog shuttle. Moel Hebog has been turned to run radiator first uphill; trials with a train consisting of three cars and the embryo coach No. 117 have indicated that, in emergency, this machine could keep time with these loaded vehicles.

No. 117, actually a Manx underframe fitted with dummy profiles to simulate the proposed bodywork, was under test for clearances. In spite of a width slightly greater than any previous coach body, no problems were encountered. The work of making the shuttle coach, No. 110, a little less open is now complete. Whether or not it will continue to operate in its priming paint this year is not yet certain. Coach No. 15, the Festiniog's - and Britain's-first bogie coach, has had a full overhaul for the first time since its major rebuild during 1958-60 and, con-

sidering the length of time involved, it is remarkable that only details needed attention.

Tunnel progress has never attained the optimum rate that, on paper at least is feasible, but steady progress was maintained up to 12th February, by which time the length of the bore was not much short of 200 metres. Then came heavy rain and a collapse of rock and boulder clay from the side of the approach cutting. To make this safe some more spoil had to be brought down, involving a diversion of the path up the old incline on to a safer alignment, and it was 25th February before work could be resumed inside the tunnel. Most of the cutting spoil was tipped at Spooner's Hollow, but a few skip-loads that appeared to consist mostly of soil rather than boulders were used to clad the embankment sides near Gelliwiog; good soil which can be seeded to blend with the landscape has never been wasted.

(left)
76.1 The weighing tables were removed from the former long loop at Minffordd early in the year, as unnecessary wear was caused to stock bumping over them. They were saved for historical reasons.

76.2 The extended railway would require a loop and signal box at Dduallt. This is the state of progress on 12th April, with the new route on the left and the old one on the right.

Summer 1976

In contrast to the opening of the 1975 season, when Rhiw Goch loop, Gelliwiog shuttle and improved Harbour Station were all hitting the headlines, this year offers little of importance to report. Traffic figures have been satisfactory without breaking records, and a large increase in sales revenue reflects the fact that the Harbour cafeteria did not open until May last year while the shops were in the throes of alterations.

It will be recalled that last year the Gelliwiog shuttle operated during Spring Bank Holiday week but not during the major part of June, as development work was needed on loco and coach. The same pattern is being followed this year, so that the new line can be kept clear for tunnel spoil trains.

A new innovation this year is an experimental Saturday evening service between Porthmadog and Penrhyn, following the withdrawal of the late Crosville bus. The train leaves Porthmadog at 22.35 and arrives back about 23.10, *Moelwyn* and two coaches being used initially. Obviously a service of this sort has to be proved viable, and members' free or privilege facilities are not available; however, the special cheap day return fare of 25p is a reasonable one.

76.3   Operation Abergele Bach took place on 22nd June. This was a joint operation with the Gwynedd Ambulance Service, Fire Service, Police, and St. John Ambulance Brigade to stage a mock accident at an awkwardly remote location near Cutting Naddu, between Penrhyn and Tan-y-bwlch.

In describing events at Boston Lodge this Spring, the cliché that immediately comes to mind is "No news is good news"; the usual pre-season tasks of routine overhaul of the locomotive fleet appeared to have been completed in nice time for battle to commence at the Spring Bank Holiday. However, just as these notes go to press comes the news that *Blanche* on 25th May suffered a major failure with the driving axle broken at the wheel seat. No serious delay to traffic occurred; although the axle-boxes had run uncomfortably warm no major fault was apparent until the wheels were actually lowered down from the engine for examination in the running shed.

During the first week in April atrocious weather failed to upset a carefully planned exercise and more than 100 tons of rails, sleepers and fastenings were unloaded on site at Buarth Melyn. About two-thirds of the tonnage came from Glan-y-Pwll and the rest from Minffordd. Drivers Higgins and Putnam performed some remarkable feats, dodging the giant Terex scrapers of the Glan-y-Don tip clearance scheme at Glan-y-Pwll and negotiating the steep curving mud-patch approach to Buarth Melyn; banking assistance was needed from the Massey Ferguson excavator on a couple of occasions and the Jones crane had to be jacked out of one treacherous soft spot.

76.4   One of the major civil engineering undertakings was the bridge over the Afon Cwmorthin, close to Tanygrisiau station. The Dow-Mac concrete beams carried useful publicity on their journey. The date is 27th July.

Autumn 1976

A correction is necessary to the notes in the last *Magazine* concerning the 22.35 Saturday night train to Penrhyn. This was only once worked by *Moelwyn* and coaches 11 and 12 (Spring Holiday Saturday). Originally the usual formation was *Upnor Castle* and the four corridor coaches which happened to be in the platform. Latterly, *Moel Hebog* push-pulling with 110 is more common. The loadings reflect the fact that the service is replacing a bus route - anything from 5 to 30 with about a dozen being most common. The bus service is being resumed in September, and it is anticipated that the train will run for the last time on 4th September.

Apart from a few trips during Spring Bank Holiday week, the Gelliwiog Shuttle has not operated this year. This was primarily to leave the new line open for the spoil trains from the tunnel to Dduallt station, but no tears were shed either by Traffic Department or Boston Lodge. The shuttle coach was very useful in the ordinary trains, in the "A" set (11.15, 13.15, 15.15, 17.15, 19.15) and if the level of traffic did not mean that it gained extra revenue, it certainly helped to reduce overcrowding and thereby sent away more satisfied passengers.

New all-steel third class coach No. 117 has been rolled out of the erecting shop into the yard regularly and as glimpsed, say, from sister 110 going by on one of the main train sets, gives the illusion of near completion. Much work remains to be done, of course, and fabrication of new and adaptation of old ex-omnibus seating is in progress inside.

76.5 With track lifted, a massive earth mover passes over Glan-y-Pwll level crossing during the transfer of slate waste to an area of marshland known as "Seven Acre Site". It was intended for the new FR terminus and was adjacent to the BR station.

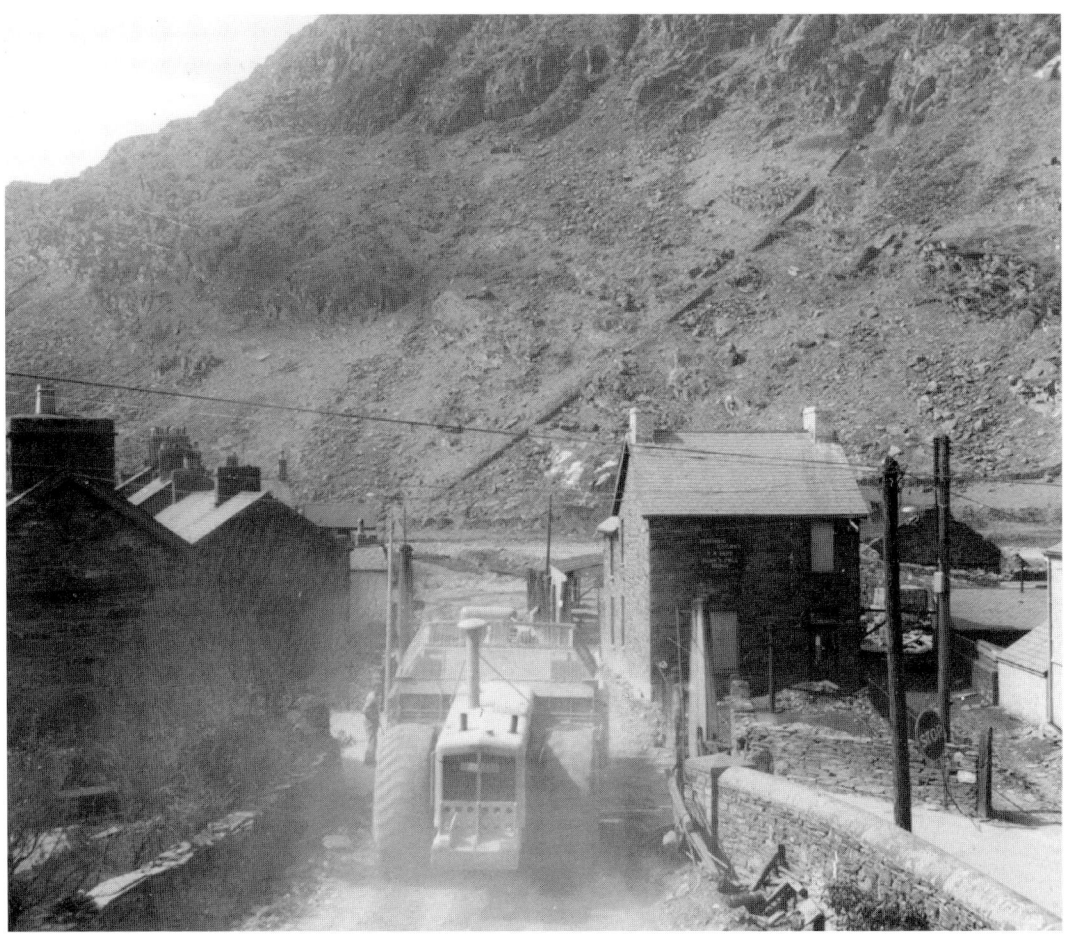

Considerable effort is being put into the Matisa tamping machine, urgently needed to consolidate the ever-increasing quantities of good granite ballast on the permanent way, particularly on the Buarth Melyn extension. Assembly of main components has not yet begun; very obvious in the shop is the simplest one of all, the roof, awaiting re-covering after a modest 10ins. has been shaved off from either side.

With the departure of Garratt K1 to York on 5th. June and the movement of the Vale of Rheidol Equipment Company's German" Bimmellbahn" 0-8-0 across the line to the old running shed, the shops during the daytime seem remarkably free of big steam except for *Earl of Merioneth*; in the absence of distraction it is pleasing to report that progress is being made here on such hidden but vital features as superheaters and fire pans.

The most spectacular happenings of the summer have been in the vicinity of the power station reception centre at Tan-y-Grisiau, by courtesy of the Civil Engineering Group's annual summer work camps. Early in July there was an onslaught on the pile of shattered rock at Tan-y-Grisiau station, spearheaded by the Smalley. The spoil was used to give good road access to the site of the Afon Cwmorthin Bridge, the abutments of which had been constructed at Easter. On 27th July a 100 ton crane was hired (actually a smaller one was ordered, but wasn't available due to a breakdown) and three articulated lorries brought in the Dow-Mac concrete beams, each 55ft. long and 3ft. high, for the crane to lift into position.

76.6   The new Moelwyn Tunnel was cut mainly by three Cornish tin miners between September 1975 and May 1976, although to less than finished dimensions. This is the south end, soon after the break through had been achieved.

76.7 A temporary terminus was required adjacent to Llyn Ystradau. The widened formation is seen in June, from a point south of the power station.

76.8 By mid-Summer, the Llyn Ystradau station site was advancing well. Intended for use in 1977 only, it would have little more than a platform edge.

77.1 A bulging embankment above Penrhyn level crossing demanded an exploratory operation in January. All structures have to be kept under observation, but few have needed such major surgery.

Winter 1976

The important effect of the extension to Llyn Ystradau is that it is no longer possible to do the round trip from Porthmadog in two hours, so that, with trains now operating on a 2½ hourly cycle, the even interval service disappears.

There has been a slight reduction in the Low Summer Monday to Friday service where, to avoid bringing in a third train set, one round trip has had to be sacrificed. A noticeable change is that the Low Summer Week-end service has been drastically reduced to enable it to be worked by one set (as in the Spring and Autumn). The second set has only ever worked in the afternoons on low summer week-ends and was never well patronised except by railtours, for whom it can still operate as required on a charter basis.

Reductions in service were not felt desirable in the peak periods and so a fourth set has to be introduced. This will be third-class only, using new stock so that, although buffet service is not advertised, a trolley service can be operated when staff is available. Timetable addicts will notice a 17.15 departure all stations to Tan-y-Bwlch (only) during the summer period - obviously a commuter train!

From 21st to 24th October, a party of Army reservists was at work between Gelliwiog and Llyn Ystradau. About 18 men of 507 STRE (Rly. Construction) under Major K. Davies camped at Capel Curig, and worked on such diverse tasks as surveying track centre lines around the new tunnel, point fitting on the main crossover at Llyn Ystradau, and laying in the loco run-round points and spur at the far end of the loop.

Although the basic trackwork at Llyn Ystradau is complete, the passenger facilities consist of an unbelievably untidy pile of rock and spoil at one end and nothing at all at the other end, while the track itself needs tamping, lining and ballasting. It is hoped that there will be time to improve the situation between completion of the Gelliwiog tamping and commencement of the tunnel tracklaying.

Spring 1977

During January, a loading ramp and approach road was constructed and the track from Llyn Ystradau extended alongside, so that the lorries could tip ballast and other materials into four or five ex-RAF wagons positioned by the Lister loco *Sludge*. Ballasting of the new line between Tunnel North Cutting and Llyn Ystradau then proceeded apace and was largely completed by 21st February.

Meanwhile, it had been decided to give rail access into the tunnel from the north. Bolster wagons loaded with rails were gingerly propelled through the tunnel to the end of the temporary track, then the rails were dragged forward with dumpers so that track laying could proceed downwards from last summer's "head of steel" near culvert 2. Connection with the tunnel track was duly completed on 1st February, and next day, in a steady downpour, the first through train from Minffordd to Llyn Ystradau was run. This consisted mainly of bolsters loaded with rails for eventual use in the tunnel. As Simplex *Jane* shed a chain that morning and none of the other small diesels was in a healthy condition, *Moel Hebog* had to propel the train through the tunnel, barging past heaps of rock and lurching ominously over the frequent lightweight jubilee points and uneven rail joints. Eventually the train was duly parked in Llyn Ystradau loop and *Moel Hebog* returned "light" (hardly an apt word in such circumstances) safely through the tunnel.

The Company's engineering consultants arranged for tunnel experts to inspect the site on 8th January, and general satisfaction was expressed with the structural aspect of the tunnel. However, in view of the nature of the rock, it was considered desirable to line the roof of the tunnel with concrete, sprayed on in two layers with mesh between, to guard against any possibility of pieces of rock becoming dislodged. This "shotcreting" will extend down the sides as well in a few places where the rock is poor. Much of the work has to be done to rigid specifications by contractors with special equipment, and it was when detailed arrangements were being made that it became apparent that trains would not be running through the tunnel early in April. As a proportion of the concrete falls on to the floor and has to be removed, it would not be practicable to lay the permanent track until after the shotcreting has been completed - there are points in favour of concrete paving, but the concrete has to be under the track, not on top of it!

77.2   This is the scene at Tunnel North in April when the shotcreting was in progress. The "torpedo" had to be hired to convey the special concrete mix from lorries at Llyn Ystradau to the pipeline in the foreground.

Summer 1977

During the Spring Bank Holiday/Jubilee week all resources were channelled into the main train service, four train sets being used between Porthmadog and Dduallt. A special half-hourly interval service was operated, totalling sixteen departures daily, but a failure to *Linda* upset the operating efficiency on the Sunday.

A minor revolution is taking place in FR train catering. To meet the needs of the fourth train set, a narrow-gauge trolley was obtained from the Enk Company in Bern, specialists in metre-gauge catering. Although intended for the newest stock, the trolley astonished the critics by negotiating the corners in the earlier corridor coaches as well, and has subsequently been used to supplement the facilities on the main trains. The saving in manpower and the attractions of impulse buying are noticeable, though we have not yet devised a way of fitting the trolley up with draught beer.

Just in the nick of time for the Festiniog's Great Leap Forward the long-awaited Matisa tamping machine has seen the light of day outside the erecting shop. On the day these notes were written, its Leyland 90h.p. diesel engine was to be run for the first time in many years, while its other complexities needed only details to be seen to. As a vehicle the machine matches other stock much better than in its days on British Rail, when it was dwarfed by normal standard-gauge rolling stock.

Locomotive mileages for 1976

	1976	Total under present administration
Prince	nil	40,287
Earl of Merioneth	nil	45,006
Merddin Emrys	5,255	43,787
Linda	10,507	77,992
Blanche	9,725	82,636
Mountaineer	3,890	47,275
Moelwyn	3,075	39,925
Upnor Castle	1,493	16,070
Moel Hebog	665	3,013
Mary Ann	1,511	14,811
Tyke	nil	180
Alistair	127	6,152
Jane	3,272	9,666
Diana	3,652	4,313
Andrew	312	480
Wickham Trolley	nil	10,212

Summer 1977 continued ....
Things began happening on 19th March, when permanent track was laid in a temporary fashion through Tunnel South cutting to join up with the temporary track in the tunnel. This enabled *Moel Hebog* to run through to Llyn Ystradau on the 20th and pick up the rail bogies which had been stored there for seven weeks. The rails were then off-loaded in the usual continuous bolted lengths, through the tunnel and slewed to one side, whereupon the old track was removed - a task which required considerably more force than was expected! Next, the "temporary" track in the south cutting was dismantled and the components slewed to one side, to enable a small tracked excavator to get into the tunnel and give a rough level for track laying. Sleepers were taken into the tunnel by dumpers on the 28th and another four days saw the permanent track laid, small but useful parties of volunteers speeding the work during both the weeks of tunnel activity.

Saturday, 28th May, saw an inspection train work through the tunnel to Llyn Ystradau. The train consisted of *Mountaineer*, wagon No. 63 and observation car No. 100. Whilst this train was at Llyn Ystradau, *Merddin Emrys* was detached from a charter special at Ddualllt and worked up to the tunnel for publicity purposes.

On Sunday, 29th May, the highlight should have been the inspection of the new line by Major P. Olver, of the Railway Inspectorate, but it became a very long day, lasting until 03.30 on Monday morning.

The inspection train (consisting of *Mountaineer*, 4 barns from the A set and wagon No. 63 sporting the new-line loading gauge) left Portmadoc at 09.45. It returned at 18.50, having been to Llyn Ystradau three times and through the tunnel four times! One Dduallt-LY trip was made for the benefit of the deviationists.

Autumn 1977

The first revenue-earning train through to Lyn Ystradau was the 15.15 on Friday afternoon, 8th July, again with *Merddin* sporting the "Blaenau Ffestiniog - Here We Come" headboard first used on the BBC train. Apart from one Saturday evening train, which was terminated at Dduallt to enable the Civil Engineering Group to attend to some bits of rock not too securely fixed in the tunnel, all trains have run through to Llyn Ystradau since, with the four-train peak service operating very smoothly. Compared with 1976 there are now two new coaches in service, and this has gone a little way towards making up for the lost capacity involved in all the trains taking longer to run the greater distances. Nevertheless, overcrowding has undoubtedly given some cause for complaint at peak hours, especially as Llyn Ystradau platform doesn't offer much in the way of home comforts for those having to wait longer than they had anticipated.

A task worthy of note undertaken recently was the recovery for our use of a quantity of flat bottom rail from the old Northern City car shed at Drayton Park North London, by members of the London Area Group. This rail is in good condition, being something under 60lb./yard weight, some of it having a 1903 rolling date. Approximately 400 track yards is now in our depot at Minffordd and will probably be used for relaying below Minffordd Quarry Lane (Lottie's) Crossing in November. The dismantling and loading was achieved in two and a half weekends, with an estimated 70 man-days work and a heroic session until 11.00 p.m. on the last day. The load eventually arrived at Porthmadog BR (rail being the only way out of the car shed) with many endearing and amusing messages painted and chalked on, which must have caused a lot of headscratching en route. This exercise was an excellent example of how volunteer labour can benefit the railway; if the lifting and loading operation had had to be paid for, the price would not have been economical to us.

Winter 1977

Not so many years ago the last fortnight in August could be relied upon to produce substantial traffic figures, often breaking both daily and weekly passenger journey records. Perhaps it's just coincidence, but since the August Bank Holiday was switched from the beginning to the end of the month the period seems to have become less popular with holidaymakers; that was certainly very obvious this year as the fortnight commencing 21st August brought some very poor returns. Fortunately things picked up again throughout the autumn period, so that bookings on the line show a small improvement on 1976's figures, but outside traffic from coach tours and BR is disappointing, and consequently the final total for the year may not be much above that for 1976. However, with the longer railway and despite the late opening of the extension, traffic revenue is up by about 27%.

Sales revenue has improved by about 13%, so that, allowing for inflation, it is more or less a case of "as you were". Very serious staff shortages have hampered progress here, particularly in the "Little Wonder" buffet, which was working reduced hours during the August peak, and in Dduallt kiosk.

The railway modelling mail order business has also tested the limits of the department's capacity during the winter months—which must be good news! At one stage orders were coming in at the rate of £200 per day. This may not sound much, but it represents a lot of brown paper and sticky tape for one person, while bringing in useful revenue at the otherwise quiet periods.

Shotcreting was scheduled to resume in the tunnel early in November, but a major setback occurred when it was found impracticable to hire the concrete transporting "torpedo" bogie wagon, which did such useful work in May and June. It was decided to construct our own, utilising an ex-Isle of Man Railway bogie coach underframe suitably strengthened, a pair of Polish bogies, a concrete mixing drum from a scrapped ready-mix lorry and a Perkins engine with hydraulic power take-off from an old gully emptier which has been tucked away in Minffordd yard for many years.

1978

Spring 1978

The Vale of Rheidol oil-firing contract has progressed steadily over the year, with a 10 sq. ft. panplate and modified burner delivered to Aberystwyth at the beginning of the year. The FR's new standard boiler (SB3) design has been completed as far as the drawing office is concerned and an order placed for construction of one boiler as a replacement for *Mountaineer's* 1918 model.

The Building Department, having finished an extension to Minffordd Station House and the complete repainting of the station block, are now working on an extension to the cafeteria stores at Harbour Station. This will incorporate needed facilities for overall-clad staff to consume acquisitions from the buffet without appearing in the public eye.

The S & T Department's work is still concentrated at Dduallt, where the Down Home signals for both main line and loop have been mounted on a bracket signal, the components for which were fabricated mainly in the new erecting shop. The Up Home signal is to be removed and the two discs used for shunting will become Homes for the main and loop line. Up Main and Down Loop starters are also being provided.

Locomotive mileages for 1977

	1977	Total under present administration
Prince	nil	40,287
Earl of Merioneth	nil	45,006
Merddin Emrys	3,965	47,756
Linda	9,613	87,605
Blanche	11,109	93,745
Mountaineer	5,396	52,671
Moelwyn	3,602	43,527
Upnor Castle	2,528	18,598
Moel Hebog	2,047	5,060
Mary Ann	970	15,781
Tyke	nil	180
Alistair	nil	6,152
Jane	3,484	13,150
Diana	1,826	6,193
Sandra	1,384	1,384
Andrew	nil	312
Sludge	100	100
Wickham Trolley	nil	10,212

Tracklaying onwards from Llyn Ystradau has proceeded rapidly. Just before Christmas a few lengths were laid on temporary formation, taking the track up on to the ballast bed being laid and vibrator rolled by MSC labour. The main task of laying to Tanygrisiau commenced on 29th December, and by the evening of the 7th January no less than 81 36ft. lengths of track had been laid, to a point just short of the Stwlan Dam road crossing.

The headache is, of course, the shotcreting of the tunnel, which has become progressively behind schedule throughout the winter, due to a variety of different problems. One was the failure of one of the two hydraulic pumps on the truck-mixer, which was rectified by obtaining a different pump. A further week's spraying was lost due to mechanical failure of the concrete pump, which involved the acquisition and fitting of a replacement winch. The theft of the battery from the truck-mixer on the Sunday evening before Christmas effectively put paid to any spraying during that week, while the freezing conditions of February complicated the all-important washing of equipment.

The biggest problems have concerned the quality of the concrete mix and the chemical admixtures used in the system. After a fortnight spent with representatives from the chemical suppliers, a satisfactory accelerator was made available to us, and during the same period the quality of the concrete mix was improved and a constant quality now appears to be available. There are some transport problems, however, and the quantity being delivered to us will need to be improved if our target is to be attained.

Summer 1978

Major Peter Olver, of the Railway Inspectorate, Department of the Environment, inspected the new line on 7th and 8th June, and authorised the Railway to operate through to Tanygrisiau as soon as certain outstanding works have been completed. He will be paying a further visit during July but has not precluded the extension of services before that visit. Subject to certain safeguards, he authorised the official opening ceremony on 24th June.

The opening did take place on 24th June, in typical Blaenau weather, and regular passenger trains to Tanygrisiau commenced the next day.

So the news from Traffic is good, but tempered by two less satisfactory aspects. The first, of course, is the frustration which has again been caused by tunnel delays; the traffic staff have taken a lot of raps from the public on this issue. Although we couldn't provide trains, we have at least opened Tanygrisiau station on weekdays from mid-May to try to minimise the backlash from passengers turning up there.

The last bit of tracklaying on the deviation had been completed by the Dee & Mersey Group on the previous week-end - a length of about 25ft which had purposely been left as late as possible to allow concrete lorries easy access to the Llyn Ystradau loading dock. The same group's Southport branch had completed the permanent track over Afon Cwmorthin bridge three weeks earlier. The whole section from above Llyn Ystradau to the top (Blaenau) end of Tanygrisiau station was tamped with the Stefcomatic on-track tamping machine in 1½ days over Easter, after several weeks' preparatory work with jacks and packing shovels.

78.1   Tanygrisiau was at last opened to traffic on 24th June 1978. A train stands in the station soon afterwards, with Cwmorthin Bridge in line with it, on the left.

Autumn 1978

Generally speaking, however, to the surprise of some and relief of others, the Tanygrisiau timetable has worked very well indeed and the timekeeping has once again been excellent. Train crews and operating staff generally must take great credit for operating this service under the most difficult of circumstances for, during the High Summer period, many trains on most weekdays have carried standing passengers in at least one direction. When services ran only to Dduallt or Llyn Ystradau, and coach parties travelled to Tan-y-Bwlch, their vacated seats could be used by short journey passengers, and it was then possible to carry over 2,500 people per day with relative ease. With most people, including parties, now going all the way, however, anything over 2,000 involves discomfort, with standing somewhere along the line, and 2,700 brings the sort of situations that traffic staff will not wish to be reminded of. Actually, the 3,000 mark has been passed on four occasions this year.

An innovation hastily introduced as a result of the peak season overcrowding was the "Early Bird" Mondays to Thursdays departure from Porthmadog at 09.00. (How many remember when 10.20 was thought to be indecently early for a tourist railway to start running?). This train allowed adults and children to travel at the children's off-peak fare-a real travel bargain-subject to the proviso that they returned from Tanygrisiau before 11.00 or after 17.00. Advance booking was encouraged, and the four basic coaches were fully booked on almost all occasions. There was a corresponding "Late Bird" facility from Tanygrisiau on the 17.13 and 17.43 scheduled trains, returning with the 19.00 from Porthmadog. The popularity of this could be judged from the number of cars parked outside the locked and deserted Tanygrisiau station in the early evening.

Work of a miscellaneous nature tackled recently includes the construction of lifting barriers for Stwlan Dam Road level crossing and water tanks for Tanygrisiau and Tan-y-Bwlch (bottom end). As a temporary measure the tank intended for Tan-y-Bwlch was erected alongside the loop line at the top (Blaenau) end of Tanygrisiau, on top of a pillar of sleepers; supports for the permanent tank have been delivered to site.

78.2   Although trains were running to Tanygrisiau, work remained to be done on two level crossings over roads that did not exist when service was "temporarily suspended" in 1939.

Winter 1978

The S & T Department have commenced installation of a new groundframe at Minffordd. Initially the frame will only operate the Porthmadog end of the station, but eventually it will be connected to the top end as well. A new groundframe is also being installed at Pen Cob so that the very cramped headshunt can be extended through the site of the present frame.

The Electrical Department has been fully extended with normal maintenance matters in recent months. They have pointed out that appreciative credit should be given to Ron Walker, of NSR Ltd., for the excellent public address equipment installed at Tanygrisiau during the summer.

During this winter's renewal programme a double milestone will be reached in the transformation of the track, this being the elimination of the old round track spike and the early, life-expired, S-shaped pattern of double-head chair, on tracks used by passenger-carrying trains. The last wholly-spiked section was removed in the autumn, when the old double-head turnout at the loop end of Minffordd crossover was replaced by a bull-head unit fabricated in the depot and towed into position on rollers.

As far as the new line is concerned, as construction ends, maintenance begins. A complete re-tamp is scheduled for the section above Llyn Ystradau, together with further crowing and alignment work, in March, to make good any settlement of the first season and ensure a track of high quality for years ahead. Additionally, there is still a considerable amount of work to be done in the new Moelwyn Tunnel, our part of the operation being to lift, ballast and tamp the track in order to dispense with the speed restriction. This work is scheduled to be completed, apart from some top ballasting, by the time these notes appear in print.

During October the department welcomed back an old friend, George Mitchell, of Thermit Welding, for a revision course on the processes he taught the longer-established members of the gang in February 1966. Previously, ex-Penrhyn Quarry Railway bull-head and ex-Barry Railway flat bottom rails have been welded, but recently the London Area Group has contributed £500 for 50 sets of materials to weld 75 lb. flat bottom-hence the revision course. Rails have been welded to span Afon Cwmorthin and Rhoslyn bridges and also to give a continuous run through Rhiw Plas bridge.

1979

Spring 1979

The Christmas service brought its interesting moments. The Harbour Station train announcements included AA road reports and mentioned roads out of the area which were still passable with extreme care. On New Year's Eve the passenger train had to wait outside Garnedd Tunnel while the engine crew hacked away the icicles, whilst on the following day the loco water facilities at Tan-y-Bwlch had frozen so solidly that *Merddin Emrys* had to run back to the 'water hole' at Boston Lodge, leaving its train for *Upnor Castle* to take on to Tanygrisiau and back after a rather cold interval. The Tan-y-Bwlch stationmaster was unkindly reminded that in the good old days (about which he is too young to remember!) braziers were lit under loco water installations. Well, times change. Whoever heard of an oil-fired brazier!

Components for new coaches 119 and 120 are forming an ever-growing pile in the new erecting shop, and hopefully the accumulation will soon begin to decrease as assembly gets under way. Construction of six new bogies is also scheduled to begin soon.

After dismantling the old works chimney, the builders have been making good the exposed area and building a new wall at the end of the machine shop/office block.

Locomotive mileages for 1978

	1978	Total under present administration
Prince	nil	40,287
Earl of Merioneth	nil	45,006
Merddin Emrys	7,911	55,663
Linda	9,654	97,259
Blanche	10,593	104,338
Mountaineer	4,240	56,911
Moelwyn	3,002	46,529
Upnor Castle	3,111	21,709
Moel Hebog	998	6,058
Mary Ann	463	16,244
Tyke	nil	180
Alistair	nil	6,152
Jane	1,476	14,626
Diana	538	6,731
Sandra	1,265	2,649
Andrew	nil	312
Sludge	87	187
Wickham Trolley	nil	10,212
Matisa Tamper	321	321

Since entering service in January 1978, the Stefcomatic on-track ballast tamper had by mid-February 1979 tamped 5¾ miles of track (this includes several sections which have been tamped twice), and the machine had performed over 14,000 tamping cycles. Although the approximate number of sleepers in 5¾ miles is only 11,400, all joints and several other sleepers are tamped twice, hence the difference in sleepers and cycles.

The policy which has evolved is to tamp new or relaid track with the machine during one winter, and to re-top and tamp again during the following winter, after a season's traffic (and the passage of about 200,000 tons of trains), thus ensuring a well consolidated final job.

79.1 One of the belated improvements at Boston Lodge this year was the provision of better staff accommodation. Those having difficulty in orientating this photograph will find the bend in the main road top left.

Summer 1979

Dick Wollan's appointment as Chief Executive of the FR in Mid-March was eclipsed in North Wales papers by the charging of seven members of the Blaenau branch of the Welsh Language Society with travelling on the railway (to wit, the Festiniog) without paying their fares. They stated that they had done so as a protest against the Company's refusal to alter its spelling (to wit, Festiniog). In correspondence the Company had previously pointed out the Parliamentary nature of its title and the consequent difficulty and expense of altering it. The WLS's spokesman described this as "a poor excuse".

After the most unpleasant winter for many years (on three occasions the train service was cut short at Tan-y-Bwlch due to snow), a mild Easter brought passengers in very encouraging numbers, so that traffic figures are just about holding their own compared with 1978. Spring bank holiday week-end, as might be expected, was something of a wash-out, but was followed by some extremely busy weekdays which brought some of the overcrowding problems experienced last August.

The Low Summer hourly-interval service with three train sets, introduced this year, seems to be meeting with general approval. It has been decided not to use the old buffet car No. 12, but instead to provide a trolley buffet

79.2 While Festiniog Travel regularly exports large numbers of its customers (albeit temporarily), it does relatively little import business. However, in August a large party of Malawi women were conveyed to Tanygrisiau. One of the temporary buildings is visible.

79.3 *Earl of Merioneth* was the first Fairlie built since 1911 and was completed in Boston Lodge in 1979. The boiler was made by Hunslets, but the bogies were existing, being two of a number moved between the double engines. The massive tanks were to improve water and fuel oil capacities.

service in the third train set formed basically of the new all-metal coaches. Research and experience (especially over Easter when buffet car No. 14 was still in shops) has shown that it is commercially preferable and more appreciated by passengers to give a limited buffet service to a large number of people rather than a complete service to a few. Full buffet services are available on all weekend and evening trains.

The new Fairlie was lowered on to its bottom bogie just before Easter and on to its top bogie in mid May, after which preparations were being made for initial tests and trials, hopefully to take place in early June. Although the bogies are basically old units, and parts of them may date back to *James Spooner* and 1872, the Fairlie is officially being considered a new engine (and thus the shell of the old engine can retain an identity of its own).

At long last the new Moelwyn tunnel looks more like a railway tunnel and a little less like a construction site. During March the bulk of the PW Department's effort was put into bringing the tunnel track up to standard which will allow the speed restriction to be removed. This work consisted of clearing sufficient shotcrete spillage from the drainage cess so that a concrete curb could be cast *in situ* throughout from portal to portal to retain the ballast. The track was then set to level and tamped with the Stefcomatic ballast tamper, slewed to alignment and the ballast topped up.

Autumn 1979

The visit of the Belgian Girl Guides to Minffordd has left the Railway short of words. Belgian Girl Guides? It sounds as unlikely a gift from heaven to the FR as Afghanistani Matchbox Collectors. But Belgian Girl Guides are not Girl Guides as we know them; they are tougher, bigger and, ha ... *older*. They camped in the oval field surrounded by the FR at Minffordd yard and had, they said afterwards, a whale of a time, tossing track about, trimming trees and driving *Moelwyn*. When we asked a permanent staff member whether they did much *work*, he looked dreamy. "Superb. A great deal. You could say there was a lot of very nice work indeed."

Traffic patterns on the "two ended railway" have begun to consolidate and there has been a very noticeable increase in the number of interchange passengers at Minffordd and Tanygrisiau. It is not uncommon for the Crosville bus company to provide three vehicles in convoy on the bus link at the northern end and it would seem that the Festiniog has become part of the transport scene. In addition, through traffic between the FR and Llechwedd has risen three-fold and that between the FR and Stwlan Dam fourteen-fold since last year. Overcrowding has again been only too common in the afternoons and it has been estimated that on an average Monday to Thursday in August about 200 passengers have to stand for at least part of their journey, very often after morning trains have run half empty.

The luxury of having five steam engines in service ended abruptly on the evening of 6th August, when *Blanche* suffered a broken axle - a repeat of the happening of 1976 - and was out of service for several weeks. The remaining four locos coped well enough, and the Works Manager resisted the temptation to try to use up the tank of particularly dirty waste oil which caused some poor performances earlier in the season.

The notable events of the early summer involved the Fairlies. The new *Earl of Merioneth* made her first trip across the Cob on 12th June, followed by modifications and running-in turns. On Saturday 23rd June she was formally named by the General Manager in a short ceremony at Harbour Station, with *Merddin Emrys* alongside sporting an 1879-1979 headboard, and on the 28th she took a 12-coach trial train through the gloom to Tanygrisiau on a damp evening, highlighting some regulator problems which were soon sorted out afterwards.

Winter 1979

Probably the most memorable event of the Autumn was the Boston Lodge open week-end, when a push-pull service ran across the Cob at approximately 15 minute intervals. Tickets were issued in the train to relieve pressure on Porthmadog booking office which was already overworked with "long distance" traffic. Including passengers for the Saturday evening buffet at the works, a total of 1780 passenger return trips were made in the one coach train, (two coaches on the first Saturday working).

Other notable happenings enlivened proceedings during October. On the 13th, Lancashire & Cheshire Railtours brought 550 passengers on the Ffestiniog Ranger day trip from Manchester, most of whom travelled on a 12 coach train hauled by the two double Fairlies.

On 17th November a special train was provided to convey the staff of Flintshire Woodlands, Mold, and their families, to Deviation sites on CEGB land where 120 trees of varieties such as oak, rowan and scots pine were planted alongside the line as a further stage of the landscaping programme. Three FR Company Directors were among 50 or so planters, but the inspired idea rounding off National Tree Week in this way was dampened by the driving rain that fell throughout the proceedings.

British Rail have introduced an exciting new circular tour this Autumn. Originating from stations within travelling distance of the FR (e.g. London, Birmingham, Manchester, Nottingham, Preston), passengers make their way by ordinary service train to Shrewsbury, thence to Porthmadog via the Cambrian Coast line. A short break for a late lunch is then taken before boarding the 15.00 FR train to Tanygrisiau, where a special bus connects into the 16.25 Conwy Valley train to Llandudno Junction. Passengers then return to their home stations by the next convenient service train.

1980

Spring 1980

A fire was lit in *Prince's* firebox on Sunday, 10th February and steam raised for the first time in more than a decade. A week's fairly intensive steam testing followed, culminating in a ballast working of more than 50 tons from Minffordd on the Saturday with the performance on a wet rail impressing all present. Passengers on the first passenger train of the season were able to get a glimpse of *Prince*, albeit in grey primer, at Tan-y-Bwlch. Some very minor adjustments are being carried out, including some efforts to improve the riding of the tender, and then the loco will be taken into the paint shop, with a view to entering service - and very useful service it should be - during April.

80.1   Dolrhedyn bridge, near the centre of Tanygrisiau, was removed by the contractors building the upper dam, with a promise of replacement when required. The council widened the road believing that the bridge would never be replaced. When the time came to honour their promises, only a Mini would have passed under it. Thus a new road was constructed to the houses above the bridge from the Stwlan Dam road. New decking was lowered in January.

Autumn 1980

Train operating has suffered at times from poor locomotive performance due to fuel problems, arising from the need to economise by burning as much waste and reprocessed oil as possible. The percentage of arrivals which are five minutes late or less has slumped from 93% in 1978 (the last time this statistic was recorded) to 82% this year. Whereas the long layovers at Tanygrisiau during the Low Summer service allow reasonable opportunities for lost time to be recovered, this year's peak timetable left little scope for recovery. An unfortunate 2% of trains have either been cancelled or have failed to reach their destination.

Earl of Merioneth was intentionally missing from the roster throughout August, while modifications were made to pan plates and fuel tanks which will hopefully improve its disappointing fuel consumption figures. Earlier some trouble with the valve face lubrication both on this locomotive and *Prince* had caused both to be out of action for some days, and *Mountaineer* had been the subject of experiments and modifications to improve performance. *Prince* and *Mountaineer* have had plenty of work to do, in addition to the two "Ladies" and *Merddin Emrys*. The re-engined *Upnor Castle* has been giving an improved performance on the "Early Bird" and, following steam failures, on other workings. The last scheduled "Early Bird" of the season on 28th August ran non-stop from Porthmadog to Tanygrisiau thanks to voluntary early starts by signalmen, one of whom walked to Dduallt in time to open the box there.

Other special events of the season included a Prince-hauled special on 17th June for the visit of BR Chairman Sir Peter Parker. After inspecting Barmouth Bridge he arrived at Minffordd BR in an inspection saloon hauled by a motor parcels van, as locomotives are not allowed over the bridge, then travelled on *Prince's* footplate to Tan-y-Bwlch before continuing to Tanygrisiau and a look at the works in hand at Blaenau.

80.2 With miles of ballast tamping to be undertaken on the new route, a machine was essential. An ex-BR tamper was skilfully converted by Steve Coulson, whose nickname was Stefco. Hence the Stefcomatic came into being.

80.3   *Princess* was placed on a plinth outside the BR terminus, to impress passengers arriving from Llandudno. In the foreground is part of Seven Acre Site, the location of the proposed FR terminus.

80.4   Various factors resulted in two new stations being built, nearer to the centre of the town. The site was photographed in May, as clearance started. Featured is the Queens Hotel, the line to Trawsfynydd passing behind it.

80.5 A welcome feature of 1980 was the provision of a carriage workshop in Glan-y-Mor Yard, adjacent to Boston Lodge. The Stefcomatic ballast tamper stands nearby.

80.6　The Development Board for Rural Wales provided substantial funding for the new work, as did the Wales Tourist Board. A special train was run in May to view progress.

80.7 The rockfall seen on page 48 necessitated a long term solution, but initially involved demolishing Penlan Cottage. This photograph from May gives an indication of the magnitude of the work.

80.8 Above the site of the stricken cottage and the trackbed was other rock of questionable stability. Much drilling was involved prior to insertion of long rock bolts in resin.

80.9 Major work was underway in Blaenau Ffestiniog in July to provide a bridge for two narrow gauge tracks under Bonar Road. The original route had been blocked when its embankment was built in 1963. The centre arch was intended for a possible passenger line to the quarries.

80.10 This and the previous picture are in opposite directions and were taken from near AA on the plan. The standard gauge track was later moved to the left. The crane was used to hoist a pneumatic hammer onto the interlocking steel sheets seen in the next picture.

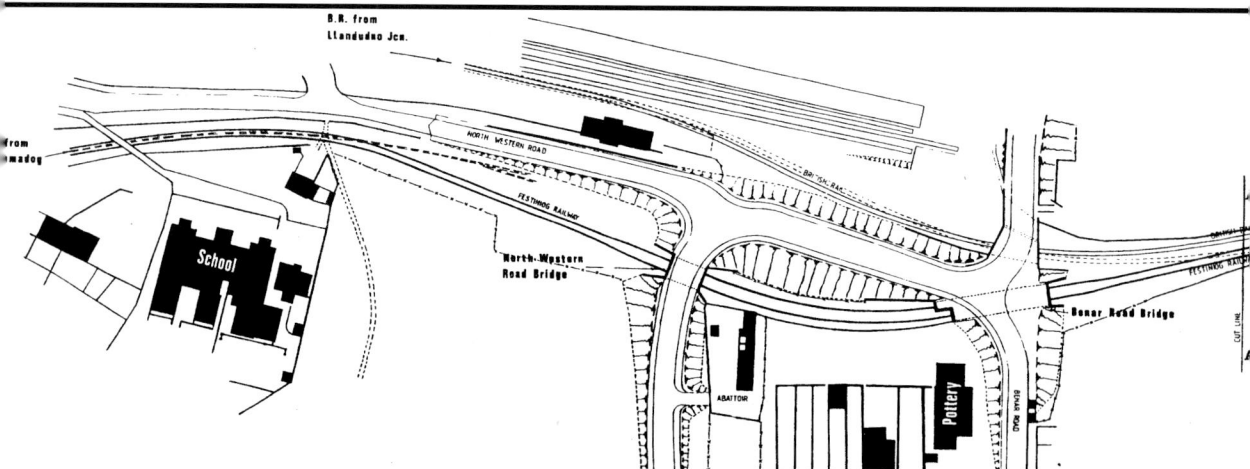

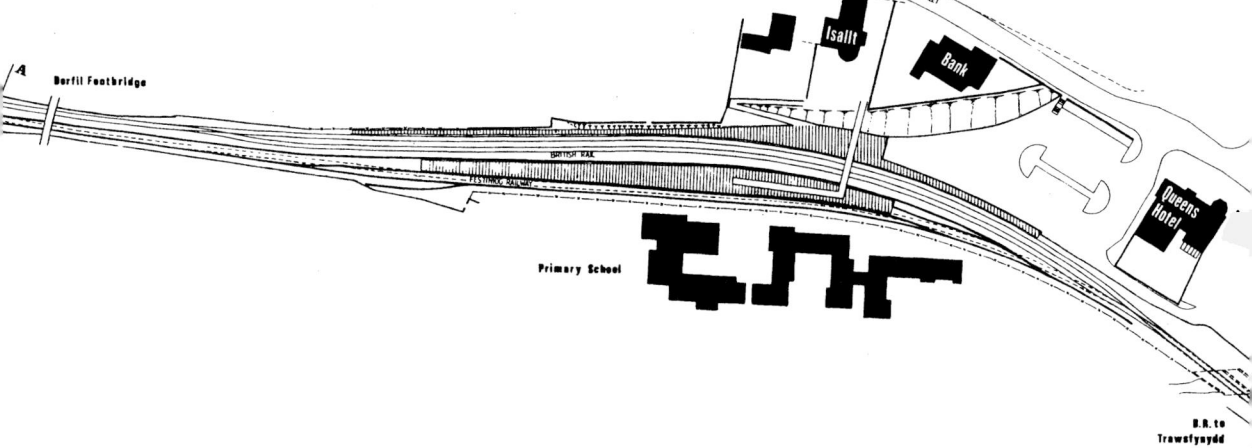

80.11 Dorfil footbridge is featured in the previous picture; its abutment is on the left of this one, which is included to show the steel sheet piling that had to be provided during the Autumn in this area of unstable ground.

1981

The complex final timetable for Tanygrisiau for a full year is worthy of study. It includes the service through to 21 March 1982, when it was hoped that the line would be reopened fully.

MILES	DATES OF OPERATION / NOTES ON FFESTINIOG RAILWAY SERVICES (SEE TABLE 1 BELOW)			SATURDAYS & SUNDAYS ONLY 14 FEBRUARY — 22 MARCH		DAILY S...			
						B		A	
0	Porthmadog ✕		d.	11 30	14 30	09{10	10 00	10{45	
	Connections from B.R. Cambrian Coast line (See notes; Table 3) NO SUNDAY SERVICE	Pwllheli	d.	1028	1210		0800sx 0737so	—	
		Barmouth	d.	—	1005	—	1323	—	0817sx 0749so
		Minffordd	a.	1058	1049	1240	1402	0830sx 0807so	0904sx 0817so
2	Minffordd ⇌		d.	11 38	14 38	"EARLY BIRD"	10 08	10{53	
3¼	Penrhyn		d.	11 45	14 45		10 15	11{00	
7½	Tan-y-Bwlch ☕		d.	12 06	15 06		10 35	11{20	
12¼	Tanygrisiau ☕		a.	12 30	15 30	10{07	11 00	11{50	
	🚌 connection by Crosville bus	Tanygrisiau Stn.	d.	1310†	1614†	10{13	1102c	12{22	
		Bl. Ffestiniog Stn.	a.	1318	1622	10{23	1112c	12{32	
	Connection to B.R. Conwy Valley line (See notes; Table 2) NO SUNDAY SERVICE X	Bl. Ffestiniog	d.	—	1625		1118g	—	
		Llandudno Jcn.	a.	—	1724		1216g	—	
		Llandudno	a.	—	1736		1229g	—	

	NOTES ON FFESTINIOG RAILWAY SERVICES (SEE TABLE 1 BELOW)					B		A	
	Connection from B.R. Conwy Valley line (See notes; Table 2) NO SUNDAY SERVICE X	Llandudno	d.	ø0750	1100	ø07{50	ø0750	10{00g	
		Llandudno Jcn.	d.	0817	1110	08{17	0817	10{10g	
		Bl. Ffestiniog	a.	0919	1212	09{18	0918	11{12g	
	🚌 connection by Crosville bus	Bl. Ffestiniog Stn.	d.	1102	1502	10{02	1050c	11{47	
		Tanygrisiau Stn.	a.	1110†	1510†	10{12	1100c	11{57	
0	Tanygrisiau ☕		d.	13 10	15 40	10{35	11 20	12{15	
4¾	Tan-y-Bwlch ☕		d.	13 30	16 00	10{55	11 40	12{35	
9	Penrhyn		d.	13 45	16 15	11{10	11 55	12{55	
10¼	Minffordd ⇌		d.	13 50	16 20	11{15	12 00	13{00	
	Connections to B.R. Cambrian Coast line (See notes; Table 3) NO SUNDAY SERVICE	Minffordd	d.	1402	1818	1647v	—	1224b	1240	1313f	1344f
		Barmouth	a.	—	—	1732v	—	—	1323	—	1420f
		Pwllheli	a.	1435	1849	—	—	1259b	—	1403f	
12¼	Porthmadog ✕		a.	14 04	16 34	11{31	12 21	13{15	

TABLE 1 — NOTES ON FFESTINIOG RAILWAY SERVICES

SPECIAL OFF PEAK FARES

Trains shown thus **10 00** are designated "off peak" and there is a very considerable reduction in fares for passengers commencing a full return journey by such trains. Except for passengers wishing to qualify for the additional "Early Bird" reduction, it is not necessary to return by the same train.

A connecting bus service operates between Tanygrisiau station, Blaenau Ffestiniog railway station and town centre, Llechwedd Caverns and Gloddfa Ganol from the beginning of April until the end of October; also between Tanygrisiau station and Stwlan Dam from mid May until mid September. See local handbills for details.

1st and 3rd Class on all trains
Picnic Site and Nature Trail at Tan-y-Bwlch
Station refreshment facilities at Porthmadog, Tan-y-Bwlch and Tanygrisiau
Wide range of souvenirs, gifts, books, etc., on sale at Porthmadog, Tan-y-Bwlch and Tanygrisiau
Model Railway Centre and Museum at Porthmadog

Agency for inland and continental bookings, reservations and enquiries at Porthmadog throughout the year.

Inclusive continental holidays by rail a speciality.
Please enquire for brochure.

{ (Printed between the hours and minutes in the timetable) indicates that the train does not operate for the full period of this section of the timetable.

A Runs Monday to Friday only 25 May to 11 Sept; also runs Sunday 24 May and Saturdays and Sundays 25 July to 30 August.

B Runs Monday to Thursday 25 May to Thursday 28 May; also Monday to Thursday only 20 July to 27 August.

C Runs Sunday 24 May to Thursday 28 May; also daily except Fridays and Saturdays 20 July to 30 August.

"Early Bird" runs as Note B. Limited capacity — advance booking essential. Continental breakfast available to passengers seats. Return adults travel at child fares, but passengers must return by same train.

X Station with self-service restaurant.
☕ Station with buffet service of light refreshments.
⇌ British Rail Cambrian Coast Line service from same station.

All trains except the 0910 ex Porthmadog call at Boston Lodge, Plas Halt, Campbell's Platform and Dduallt on request. To board, passengers must give a hand signal to the driver. To alight, please give notice to the guard on boarding.

For Easter Saturday, Sunday and Monday additional trains will operate. (See local announcements.) At other times additional trains will operate according to demand.

To assist punctuality at busy times the booking office will close five minutes before departure time.

CROSVILLE BUS CONNECTIONS (Tanygrisiau — Blaenau Ffestiniog)
c Mondays to Saturdays; also Sundays 24 May to 30 August.
• Mondays to Saturdays; also Sundays 24 May and 19 July to 30 August (on Sundays 31 May to 12 July also 6 September runs 14 mins later).
† Bus operates from Tanygrisiau (Dolydd Terrace). This service is shown for information only. IT DOES NOT OPERATE ON SUNDAYS.

RDAY 28 MARCH TO SUNDAY 1 NOVEMBER

SATS & SUNS 7, 8 NOV.; 19, 20 DEC.
DAILY 26 DEC. TO 3 JAN. 1982. SATS
& SUNS 13 FEB. TO 21 MARCH 1982

A	A	A	A	A	B	C		
35	12 30	13 20	14 10	15 00	15 55	16 45	19 00	11 30	14 30
—	1030	—	1210	—	1314f	—	1339w	—	1507f	—	1630h	—	1710	—	1030	—	1210	—
1005	—	1005	—	1232f	—	—	—	1323	—	1524	—	1731	—	1005	—	1323
1005	1100	1140b	1240	1313f	1344f	1412w	1402	1537f	1647h	1611	1740	1815	1100	1049	1240	1402
1049		1049														
		1224b														
43	12 38	13 28	14 18	15 08	16 03	16 53	19 08	11 38	14 38
50	12 45	13 35	14 25	15 15	16 10	17 00	19 15	11 45	14 45
10	13 05	13 55	14 45	15 35	16 30	17 20	19 35	12 05	15 05
40	13 30	14 20	15 10	16 00	16 51	17 41	19 57	12 30	15 30
45	1337c	14 33	15 22	1608e	16 55	17 57	20 44†	1310†	1614†
55	1347c	14 43	15 32	1618e	17 05	18 07	20 52	1320	1624
1327k	—	14 50g	—	1625	17 50fg	2015j 2020p	21 42p	1327	1625
1428k		15 48g		1723	18 48fg	2116j 2118p	22 40p	1428	1723
1438k		15 58g		1733	19 10fg	— ø2224p	22 50p	1438	1733

A	A	A	A	A	B	C		
1105q	z 1208g	—	13 35g	1454	—	16 24p	17 55	ø0750	1105
1115q	z 1218g	—	13 45g	1504	—	16 35p	18 05	0817	1115
1216q	z 1321g	—	14 46g	1607	—	17 42p	19 07	0918	1216
32	1327c	14 32	15 17	1612c	16 42	17 47	19 27	1155	1500
42	1337c	14 42	15 27	1622c	16 52	17 57	19 35†	1210†	1510†
05	13 50	14 45	15 35	16 25	17 20	18 00	20 05	13 10	15 40
25	14 10	15 05	16 00	16 45	17 40	18 20	20 25	13 30	16 00
45	14 25	15 25	16 20	17 05	17 55	18 35	20 45	13 50	16 20
50	14 30	15 30	16 25	17 10	18 00	18 40	20 50	13 55	16 25
1412w	1611	—	1611	1537t	—	1647h	1815	1740r	1815	—	—	2040	2200	—	1402	—	1815	1647
1449w	—	—	—	1620t	—	1730h	—	1826r	—	—	—	2117	—	—	—	1730
—	1650	1650	—	—	1842	1842	—	—	2228	—	1429	1842	—
05	14 55	15 45	16 40	17 30	18 16	18 54	21 00	14 05	16 35

Advance booking is essential on these dates.

FATHER CHRISTMAS will meet the trains on 19 and 20 December to distribute presents to the children.

 BRITISH RAIL CONNECTIONAL SERVICES TABLES 2 & 3

TABLE 2 — CONWY VALLEY LINE
(Blaenau Ffestiniog — Llandudno & v.v.)

- ø — Change at Llandudno Junction.
- f — Saturdays only 25 July to 29 August.
- g — Mondays to Fridays only 15 June to 4 September.
- j — Mondays to Fridays only 25 to 29 May.
- k — From 1 June.
- p — Mondays to Thursdays only 20 July to 27 August.
- q — Mondays to Fridays only, 1 to 12 June and 7 to 11 September also Saturdays only 25 July to 29 August.
- z — Until 30 May Llandudno dep. 1100, Llandudno Junction dep. 1110, Blaenau Ffestiniog arr. 1212. From 1 June, EXCEPT Mondays to Fridays 15 June to 4 September Llandudno dep. 1105, Llandudno Jcn. dep. 1115, Blaenau Ffestiniog arr. 1216.
- ✻ — On certain summer Sundays "Super Sunday Shuttles" operate on this line. See special handbills.

TABLE 3 — CAMBRIAN COAST LINE
(Pwllheli — Barmouth & v.v.)

- so — Saturdays only.
- sx — Mondays to Fridays only.
- b — Saturdays only 6 June to 19 September; also Wednesdays only 8 July to 2 September.
- f — Saturdays only 25 July to 29 August.
- h — Not on schooldays.
- r — Mondays to Fridays; also Saturdays 24 May to 19 September.
- t — Schooldays only.
- v — Until the re-opening of Barmouth Viaduct, Minffordd dep. 1740, Barmouth arr. 1824.
- w — Wednesdays only 8 July to 2 September.

of the Great Little Trains of Wales

Spring 1981

For the weekend of 4-5th April the FR Company is offering free third class travel on the railway to all residents of Porthmadog, Penrhyndeudraeth and Blaenau Ffestiniog areas. There are many people living in the area who have never travelled on the line, and the invitations are being sent out in the interests of furthering relations between the FR and its neighbours. The normal train services will run during the week-end.

On 28th February a start was made above Tanygrisiau, when several lengths of track were laid through the cutting to enable materials trains to be propelled clear of the "one engine in steam" operating section during April, when work should commence on tracklaying to connect with the existing track beyond Penlan. Ballast will be brought in by road to the old Cwmorthin Siding site, and from there carried by dumper along the formation to lay a ballast bed. Tracklaying is planned to follow, to give rail access to Barlwyd Bridge by the end of May to facilitate its reconstruction.

Some of the larger culverts and underpasses have been uncovered, ready for additional concrete decking to be poured over the original slate ones, or to be reinforced with concrete sleepers. Sheffield Group have piped what was believed to be an unnecessarily large culvert but which turned out to have been a coal chute!

81.1 As all thoughts were on completing the line, a problem arose close to Boston Lodge. The subsidence at Bron Madoc crossing was photographed in bad weather on 11th March.

81.2 The site behind the Queens Hotel had only a distant signal as evidence of railway use in March. The area once had a fan of GWR sidings, but latterly only a single track to Trawsfynydd. That would soon be relaid on the left of this eastward view.

81.3 New ballast was approaching the Queens Hotel in April. New BR track would be laid on the left during the following month, using a road crane to lift track panels off a train standing on the right.

Summer 1981

Just a day too late for mention in the last *Magazine*, extremely heavy rain caused the failure of an embankment just by the main road above the upper Boston Lodge cottages, in the early hours of 11th March, when a 30ft section of bank subsided due to flood water from adjacent high ground washing away the sub-strata of sand on to the main road. A long day's work on the Friday by both PW and CEG departments saw the track supported on timbers for the safe passage of the Saturday and all subsequent trains, albeit at a strict 5 mph. This situation will remain for the rest of the season and remedial works will be undertaken during the winter.

During the early Spring, there have been several clearing up sessions on the New Line as well as a modicum of further peat spreading. Above Tanygrisiau, the first two footbridges have been demolished. Heightening of the abutments of the one near the station has been completed and a good deal of additional side walling has been built (Lancs. & Cheshire Group members). A temporary bridge now spans the site and this will be used partly to help form the new concrete structure. At the second footbridge, the abutments are in course of being heightened (Midland Group). A ballast wharf with a concrete apron has been erected at the end of the approach road to the former Cwmorthin Sidings. More than a thousand tons will have to be transhipped here before the line reopens.

The Central Station scheme is by no means finished but all the roads in Blaenau were fully reopened for Easter. BR have laid new track at their station site and taken up the old, so that our station area can be excavated, but standard gauge track still covers our formation either side of Dorfil bridge, though this should soon be cleared. With the BR hired (road) crane out of the way, erection of the station footbridge can now proceed. Up here too, there is still much stone walling to be built, as well as the laying out of pavements, car parks, street lighting and so on.

81.4   Special concrete beams were installed during April at the Penlan rockfall site. The retaining wall was thus secure under the track. The earlier views are on pages 48, 71 and 72.

FESTINIOG RAILWAY LOCOMOTIVE STOCK AND 1980 MILEAGES

Locomotive	Type & Building Details	1980 miles	Total (FR since 1955)
Prince	0-4-0STT, Geo. England 1863	4,761	45,048
Merddin Emrys	0-4-4-0T, Fairlie, Boston Lodge 1879	6,662	70,560
Earl of Merioneth/ Iaril Meirionydd	0-4-4-0T Fairlie, Boston Lodge 1979	5,524	8,634
Linda	2-4-0STT, Hunslet (590) 1893	11,424	120,534
Blanche	2-4-0STT, Hunslet (589) 1893	5,761	119,287
Mountaineer	2-6-2T, Alco (57156) 1916	2,938	63,709
(Volunteer)	0-6-0ST, Peckett (2050) 1944	under investigation for rebuild	
Princess	0-4-0STT, Geo. England 1863	displayed at Harbour Station Museum	
(Welsh Pony)	0-4-0STT, Geo. England 1867	out of service	
(Livingston Thompson)	0-4-4-0T, Fairlie, Boston Lodge 1886	body stored pending display	
Kl	0-4-0 + 0-4-0, Garratt, Beyer Peacock (5792)1909	on loan to N.R.M. York	
Britomart	0-4-0ST, Hunslet (707) 1899	privately owned	
Mary Ann	4wDM Simplex, Motor Rail (596?) 1917	104	16,643
Moelwyn	2-4-0DM, Baldwin (49604) 1918	971	49,954
Upnor Castle	4wDM Planet, Hibberd (9687) 1954	2,068	25,958
	4wDM Planet, Hibberd (3831) 1957	awaiting rebuild	
Moel Hebog	0-4-0DM mines, Hunslet (4113) 1956	702	8,136
(Jane)	4wDM Simplex, Motor Rail (8565) 1940	678	15,251
The Lady Diana	4wDM Simplex, Motor Rail (21579) 1957	30	6,761
(Sandra)	4wDM Motor Rail (22119) 1962	2,736	6,121
Tyke	4wDM Hunslet (2290) 1941	out of service	
Alistair	4wDM Ruston (201970) 1940	nil	6,152
Andrew	4wDM Ruston (193984) 1939	out of service	
(Sludge)	4wDM Lister (41545) 1954	out of service	
-	2-2-0PM Wickham trolley	out of service	
Stefcomatic	2-2-0DH Matisa tamper	119	686
-	4wDM Simplex, Motor Rail (8788) 1943	privately owned by Col. Campbell	

Note: 4w denotes driving axles connected by chains.

81.5 New rail is being positioned above Tanygrisiau early in 1981.

81.6 A fine line up was recorded from "head office" in April. *Prince* is in steam, while behind it is *Palmerston* coupled to *Mountaineer* and *Merddin Emrys*.

Autumn 1981

With the completion (to a state ready for track to be laid) of the new Afon Barlwyd Bridge being achieved just in time, work began on 1st August on relaying the track from just below the bridge to Glanypwll depot. This involved the lifting of the last remaining section of undisturbed old track on the main line, the bull-head rail being good enough for re-use. It has been stored at Tan-y-Bwlch for using at Penrhediad in 1983.

Winter 1981

A major change is taking place in the railway's phone system. The exchange at Boston Lodge is being replaced by entirely fresh Tandem equipment, obtained free but since extensively overhauled. This becomes the central feature of the whole automatic installation. At the same time, Penrhyn exchange has been dispensed with and its extensions transferred to Minffordd. The other local exchanges will in future be at Porthmadog, Tan-y-Bwlch, Dduallt and Glanypwll. All calls between any of these will be routed via Boston Lodge. The difference apparent to anyone using an extension is that, instead of dialling 29 to link into each exchange successively along the line, making it a cumbersome procedure to call one end from the other, only four digits need be dialled, no matter how far away is the extension being called.

By the beginning of November, a ballast track bed had been laid through our platform at Central station and down Dorfil Bridge cutting, under Bonar Road and the A496 bridges, almost to Glanypwll level crossing. Below the crossing, permanent track was in place to a point a little short of it, with the crossover into the depot laid and tamped, but much work still needed on drainage, ballasting and packing. A start of ballasting of the 60lb. rail length was made on 7th November, those places requiring considerable adjustment to cant being ballasted first. However, the bulk of this work will be left until the New Year, the time up till Christmas being taken up on construction of the Central Station pointwork (at Minffordd) and other preparations.

1982

Spring 1982

The maintenance programme announced in the last Magazine has been largely completed, with a little 'after sales service' required early in the new season at Penrhyn, completion of some outstanding brickwork in Garnedd tunnel, due to the cold weather in December freezing the inside of the tunnel, and various small tamping jobs requiring attention.

A week has been spent, from 30th January, at Bron Madoc, realigning the track, by about 4 feet, into an 'S' bend around the slip site. This requires a pair of slightly longer rails to be welded and placed in the track and a retamp after a little traffic, at the end of March, with a view to removing the 5 mph Temporary Speed Restriction in May. Otherwise, most of the Department's effort has been in the construction of the new section to Blaenau Ffestiniog and this will continue to absorb our resources until May.

Locomotive	1981	Total (FR since 1955)	Locomotive	1981	Total (FR since 1955)
Linda	7,285	127,819	Mary Ann	51	16,694
Mountaineer	779	64,488	Jane	973	16,224
Merddin Emrys	6,813	77,373	The Lady Diana	288	7,049
Blanche	9,484	128,771	Sandra	657	6,778
Earl of Merioneth	6,045	14,679	Upnor Castle	2,329	28,287
Prince	4,400	49,448	Moel Hebog	170	8,306
Moelwyn	1,595	51,549	Matisa	188	874

Locomotives not listed performed no mileage during 1981.

82.1 Although nuclear flask trains to Trawsfynydd ran only a few times per month, a footbridge was demanded. This was the first structure built on what was still known as "Blaenau Central". Heavy snow in January hampered track laying.

82.2 Footbridge rebuilding was undertaken mainly by Society Groups. Numbered from the south, this is no. 4 at Groesffordd, near Glan-y-Pwll which is in the background. The new concrete deck was poured in March.

82.3   Re-opening day was only weeks away as great effort was made to complete track relaying over Glan-y-Pwll level crossing in February. See page 54 for the same location in 1976. With a road closure order, all traffic was diverted onto the new road.

82.4　The BR station opened on 22nd March and its first train was accompanied by *Blanche* whistling on the parallel track from the old station. The DMU was then moved onto the loop line to allow a nuclear flask train to pass.

82.5 A close-up of the headboard is a reminder that the quickest way between Porthmadog and London would soon be via this route. There had been good cooperation between all the authorities concerned.

82.6 During March, the FR's loop was completed, but some of the secondhand rails had dropped ends. This device was used to bend them back up again to give a smooth ride and reduce maintenance.

82.7 A symbolic load of slate from Llechwedd Quarry was conveyed to Porthmadog. Traditional loading is seen, but a lorry had to be used to take the wagons to the FR, at Glan-y-Pwll.

82.8 A special slate train was operated on 19th May, ahead of re-opening to passengers. *Prince* returns to almost its original role; it was initially intended to only haul empty wagons back to the town by steam.

82.9 Some tarmac was down, but many finishing touches were required before opening day. The BR building, with its traditional yellow brick quoins, was complete, but the FR had to use some sheds temporarily.

82.10 Opening day was a memorable occasion with flags waving from and at the first train, as it ran past the houses on its approach to the town. Supporters of all ages packed both platforms.

82.11 The euphoria of the re-opening continued, as two special trains arrived on Sunday 6th June. One was organised by Linkwise Tours and originated at Euston. It is in the loop after discharging its passengers, while the FR train stands at a totally bald platform.

Autumn 1982

25th May came and went with more than the usual splash of rain, but this did not seem to deter the crowds or affect their enjoyment of the memorable occasion. The 09.55 from Porthmadog ran (almost 'by the way') to Tanygrisiau and thereafter all trains went through to Blaenau. The 10.10 ex Porthmadog and 12.00 ex Blaenau carried invited guests only - two separate groups in fact. The first group detrained at Blaenau and returned at 12.50 with another train which had arrived empty, whilst the other group made a round trip from the Blaenau end. This 12.00 train, incidentally, ran non-stop to Porthmadog in 52 minutes. Thereafter, there were medal holders to be carried and a rather larger number than usual of ordinary passengers for a wet Tuesday in May. A modified low-summer service was operated with a last departure from Blaenau at 17.53.

There has been an enormous increase in bookings from British Rail stations to the FR. In the 4 weeks ending 12th.June, this traffic increased threefold compared with 1981.

A significant proportion of FR traffic, probably about 8%, is using the train as a means of genuine public transport. Most of these passengers are travelling to and from Wales at the start and finish of their holidays, or using the 'Link' as an interesting and convenient way of going from North to Mid Wales or vice versa. A much smaller, though nevertheless important number, are local people finding that it is easier to catch a train to Llandudno Junction than to motor to Bangor.

The FR joined British Rail's Red Star parcels network on 9th August. Parcels are conveyed outwards from Porthmadog by the 12.25 train on Mondays to Fridays, for same day arrival in London, Manchester or other stations with direct rail service from Llandudno Junction, or next morning arrival in other parts of Britain. The livery of the sliding doors of coaches 100 and 101 has been modified to include an adaptation of BR's famous Red Star - in our case in FR cherry red with an FR crest replacing the double arrow logo. The star is set on a cream background, with the words 'Parcels Service' beneath.

82.12 The Steam Locomotive Operators Association train was used for the "Festiniog Pullman" from Crewe via Manchester. Demand was so great that it ran again on 12, 13 and 20 June, special trains being provided to Porthmadog. The FR had its first booking office in a former private house nearby, shared with the Tourist Information Centre and named "Isallt". Success was achieved 31 years after the formation of the Festiniog Railway Society in Bristol in 1951. Your authors were there and still marvel at the subsequent efforts of so many supporters.

X. List of coaches in 1981. The locomotive list is on page 81.

Bogie Coaches

No.	Builder	Date	Compartments from top end	Seating 3rd	Seating 1st	Notes
10	Brown Marshalls	1872	3/3/G	12		Awaiting rebuilding
11	Brown Marshalls	1880	G/1/1 obs	—	15	
12	Brown Marshalls	1880	3 sal buf	22		
14	Bristol	1898	3 sal buf	23		ex L. & B. reb. BL 1963
15	Brown Marshalls	1871	3/3/3/1/3/3/3	48	6	
16	Brown Marshalls	1871	3/3/3/1/1c/3/3	40	9	1st coupé compartment
17	Brown Marshalls	1876	3/3/1/3/3/3	40	6	⎫
18	Brown Marshalls	1876	3/3/1/3/3/3	40	6	⎬ Bow siders
19	Gloster	1879	3/3/1/1/3/3	32	12	
20	Gloster	1879	3/3/1/1/3/3	32	12	⎭
22	Ashbury	1896	seven 3rds	56		⎫
23	Ashbury	1894	seven 3rds	56		⎬ ex WHR
26	Ashbury	1894	seven 3rds	56		⎭
37	Boston Lodge	1971	3/3/3/3	32		Hudson frame (ex 70)
38	Boston Lodge	1971	3/3/3/3	32		Hudson frame (ex 66)
100	Boston Lodge	1965	G/1 sal/1 obs		18	⎫
101	Boston Lodge	1970	G/1 sal/1 obs		18	⎬
103	Boston Lodge	1968	buf/ 3 sal	17		body components
104	Boston Lodge	1964	3 sal/1/3 sal	32	4	prefabricated by H. L. Watson
105	Boston Lodge	1966	3 sal/1/3 sal/lav	29	4	
106	Boston Lodge	1968	3 sal/1/3/sal	32	4	⎭
110	Boston Lodge	1975	3 sal/auto	42		with ex Polish State Rlys. Diamond Frame Bogies
116	Edmund Crow	1972	3 sal/1	32	4	
117	Boston Lodge	1977	3 sal	39		Ex I-o-M Rly. Underframe
118	Boston Lodge	1977	3 sal	39		,, ,, ,, ,,
119	Boston Lodge	1980	3 sal/lav	32		,, ,, ,, ,,
120	Boston Lodge	1980	3 sal/lav	32		,, ,, ,, ,,
121	Boston Lodge	1981	3 sal	39		,, ,, ,, ,,

Four-wheeled coaches

No.	Built	Compartments	3rd seats	Notes
1	1964	Open	8	Pass. brake van built Midland Group
2	18??	Open	6	Goods brake van
3	1864-7	Knifeboard	14	Closed
4	1864-7	Knifeboard	14	Closed
5	1864-7	Knifeboard	14	Closed. Rebuilt by R. G. Jarvis
6	1864-7	Knifeboard	14	Open. Under rebuild by R. G. Jarvis
7	1864-7	Knifeboard	14	Open. Displayed at Harbour Station Museum
8	187?	Open	14	Quarrymen's coach
59	192?	Open	—	Luggage/stores van. formerly W. & L. sheep van

Middleton Press

Easebourne Lane, Midhurst, W Sussex. GU29 9AZ Tel: 01730 813169 Fax: 01730 812601
If books are not available from your local transport stockist, order direct with cheque, Visa or Mastercard, post free UK.

BRANCH LINES
Branch Line to Allhallows
Branch Line to Alton
Branch Lines around Ascot
Branch Line to Ashburton
Branch Lines around Bodmin
Branch Line to Bude
Branch Lines around Canterbury
Branch Lines around Chard & Yeovil
Branch Line to Cheddar
Branch Lines around Cromer
Branch Lines to East Grinstead
Branch Lines of East London
Branch Lines to Effingham Junction
Branch Lines around Exmouth
Branch Line to Fairford
Branch Lines around Gosport
Branch Line to Hawkhurst
Branch Lines to Horsham
Branch Lines around Huntingdon
Branch Line to Ilfracombe
Branch Line to Kingswear
Branch Lines to Launceston & Princetown
Branch Lines to Longmoor
Branch Line to Looe
Branch Line to Lyme Regis
Branch Lines around March
Branch Lines around Midhurst
Branch Line to Minehead
Branch Line to Moretonhampstead
Branch Lines to Newport
Branch Lines around North Woolwich
Branch Line to Padstow
Branch Lines around Plymouth
Branch Lines to Seaton and Sidmouth
Branch Line to Selsey
Branch Lines around Sheerness
Branch Line to Shrewsbury
Branch Line to Swanage updated
Branch Line to Tenterden
Branch Lines around Tiverton
Branch Lines to Torrington
Branch Lines to Tunbridge Wells
Branch Line to Upwell
Branch Lines of West London
Branch Lines around Weymouth
Branch Lines around Wimborne
Branch Lines around Wisbech

NARROW GAUGE
Branch Line to Lynton
Branch Lines around Portmadoc 1923-46
Branch Lines around Porthmadog 1954-94
Branch Line to Southwold
Douglas to Port Erin
Kent Narrow Gauge
Two-Foot Gauge Survivors
Romneyrail
Southern France Narrow Gauge
Vivarais Narrow Gauge

SOUTH COAST RAILWAYS
Ashford to Dover
Bournemouth to Weymouth
Brighton to Eastbourne
Brighton to Worthing
Dover to Ramsgate
Eastbourne to Hastings
Hastings to Ashford
Portsmouth to Southampton
Ryde to Ventnor
Southampton to Bournemouth

SOUTHERN MAIN LINES
Basingstoke to Salisbury
Bromley South to Rochester
Crawley to Littlehampton
Dartford to Sittingbourne
East Croydon to Three Bridges
Epsom to Horsham
Exeter to Barnstaple
Exeter to Tavistock
Faversham to Dover
London Bridge to East Croydon
Orpington to Tonbridge
Tonbridge to Hastings
Salisbury to Yeovil
Swanley to Ashford
Tavistock to Plymouth
Victoria to Bromley South
Victoria to East Croydon
Waterloo to Windsor
Waterloo to Woking
Woking to Portsmouth
Woking to Southampton
Yeovil to Exeter

EASTERN MAIN LINES
Ely to Kings Lynn
Fenchurch Street to Barking
Ipswich to Saxmundham
Liverpool Street to Ilford

WESTERN MAIN LINES
Ealing to Slough
Exeter to Newton Abbot
Newton Abbot to Plymouth
Paddington to Ealing
Plymouth to St. Austell
Slough to Newbury

COUNTRY RAILWAY ROUTES
Andover to Southampton
Bath Green Park to Bristol
Bath to Evercreech Junction
Bournemouth to Evercreech Jn.
Cheltenham to Andover
Croydon to East Grinstead
Didcot to Winchester
East Kent Light Railway
Fareham to Salisbury
Frome to Bristol
Guildford to Redhill
Reading to Basingstoke
Reading to Guildford
Redhill to Ashford
Salisbury to Westbury
Stratford upon Avon to Cheltenham
Strood to Paddock Wood
Taunton to Barnstaple
Wenford Bridge to Fowey
Westbury to Bath
Woking to Alton
Yeovil to Dorchester

GREAT RAILWAY ERAS
Ashford from Steam to Eurostar
Clapham Junction 50 years of change
Festiniog in the Fifties
Festiniog in the Sixties
Isle of Wight Lines 50 years of change
Railways to Victory 1944-46
Return to Blaenau 1970-82
SECR Centenary album
Talyllyn 50 years of change
Yeovil 50 years of change

LONDON SUBURBAN RAILWAYS
Caterham and Tattenham Corner
Charing Cross to Dartford
Clapham Jn. to Beckenham Jn.
Crystal Palace (HL) & Catford Loop
East London Line
Finsbury Park to Alexandra Palace
Kingston and Hounslow Loops
Lewisham to Dartford
Lines around Wimbledon
London Bridge to Addiscombe
Mitcham Junction Lines
North London Line
South London Line
West Croydon to Epsom
West London Line
Willesden Junction to Richmond
Wimbledon to Beckenham
Wimbledon to Epsom

STEAMING THROUGH
Steaming through Cornwall
Steaming through the Isle of Wight
Steaming through Kent
Steaming through West Hants
Steaming through West Sussex

TRAMWAY CLASSICS
Aldgate & Stepney Tramways
Barnet & Finchley Tramways
Bath Tramways
Bournemouth & Poole Tramways
Brighton's Tramways
Bristol's Tramways
Burton & Ashby Tramways
Camberwell & W.Norwood Tramways
Clapham & Streatham Tramways
Croydon's Tramways
Dover's Tramways
East Ham & West Ham Tramways
Edgware and Willesden Tramways
Eltham & Woolwich Tramways
Embankment & Waterloo Tramways
Enfield & Wood Green Tramways
Exeter & Taunton Tramways
Greenwich & Dartford Tramways
Hammersmith & Hounslow Tramways
Hampstead & Highgate Tramways
Hastings Tramways
Holborn & Finsbury Tramways
Ilford & Barking Tramways
Kingston & Wimbledon Tramways
Lewisham & Catford Tramways
Liverpool Tramways 1. Eastern Routes
Liverpool Tramways 2. Southern Routes
Liverpool Tramways 3. Northern Routes
Maidstone & Chatham Tramways
Margate to Ramsgate
North Kent Tramways
Norwich Tramways
Portsmouth's Tramways
Reading Tramways
Seaton & Eastbourne Tramways
Shepherds Bush & Uxbridge Tramways
Southampton Tramways
Southend-on-sea Tramways
Southwark & Deptford Tramways
Stamford Hill Tramways
Twickenham & Kingston Tramways
Victoria & Lambeth Tramways
Waltham Cross & Edmonton Tramways
Walthamstow & Leyton Tramways
Wandsworth & Battersea Tramways

TROLLEYBUS CLASSICS
Croydon Trolleybuses
Bournemouth Trolleybuses
Hastings Trolleybuses
Maidstone Trolleybuses
Reading Trolleybuses
Woolwich & Dartford Trolleybuses

WATERWAY ALBUMS
Kent and East Sussex Waterways
London to Portsmouth Waterway
Surrey Waterways
West Sussex Waterways

MILITARY BOOKS
Battle over Portsmouth
Battle over Sussex 1940
Bombers over Sussex 1943-45
Bognor at War
Military Defence of West Sussex
Military Signals from the South Coast
Secret Sussex Resistance
Surrey Home Guard
Sussex Home Guard

OTHER RAILWAY BOOKS
Index to all Middleton Press stations
Industrial Railways of the South-East
South Eastern & Chatham Railways
London Chatham & Dover Railway
War on the Line (SR 1939-45)

BIOGRAPHIES
Garraway Father & Son
Mitchell & company